Ours

Ours

The Case for Universal Property

Peter Barnes

polity

First published in 2021 by Polity Press

Polity Press
65 Bridge Street
Cambridge CB2 1UR, UK

Polity Press
101 Station Landing
Suite 300
Medford, MA 02155, USA

ISBN-13: 978-1-5095-4482-0 (hardback)
ISBN-13: 978-1-5095-4483-7 (paperback)

A catalogue record for this book is available from the British Library.

Library of Congress Cataloging-in-Publication Data

Names: Barnes, Peter, 1942- author.
Title: Ours : the case for universal property / Peter Barnes.
Description: Cambridge, UK ; Medford, MA : Polity Press, 2021. | Includes bibliographical references and index. | Summary: "How we can rewire private property to work for people, not corporations"-- Provided by publisher.
Identifiers: LCCN 2021000325 (print) | LCCN 2021000326 (ebook) | ISBN 9781509544820 (hardback) | ISBN 9781509544837 (paperback) | ISBN 9781509544844 (epub)
Subjects: LCSH: Property. | Equality.
Classification: LCC HB701 .B367 2021 (print) | LCC HB701 (ebook) | DDC 330.1/7--dc23
LC record available at https://lccn.loc.gov/2021000325
LC ebook record available at https://lccn.loc.gov/2021000326
Typeset in 12/15 Fournier MT by
Servis Filmsetting Ltd, Stockport, Cheshire
Printed and bound in Great Britain by TJ Books Ltd, Padstow, Cornwall

For further information on Polity, visit our website: politybooks.com

Contents

Acknowledgments

I could not have written this book without the continued love and support of my partner, Cornelia Durrant.

Others who inspired me with ideas and feedback include Marcellus Andrews, William Arnone, Joseph Blasi, David Bollier, Matthew Bruenig, Robert Costanza, Gus diZerega, Layla Forrest-White, Natalie Foster, Robert Friedman, John Fullerton, John Garn, Sam Hammond, Robert Hockett, Alex Howlett, Chris Hughes, Edward Kirshner, George Lakoff, Mary Lehmann, Wendy McLaughlin, Christopher Mackin, Ioana Marinescu, David Morris, Griffin Murphy, Janelle Orsi, George Owers, Lenore Paladino, Richard Parker, Brent Ranalli, Mike Sandler, Scott Santens, Jeremy Sherman, Fraser Murison Smith, Gus Speth, Guy Standing, Marshall Steinbaum, Steve Randy Waldman, Karl Widerquist, and David Sloan Wilson. In addition, I am grateful to Tom White and the Vedanta Society of Northern California for providing me with beautiful spaces to think and write.

I am also deeply indebted to a long line of original thinkers, including Thomas Paine, Henry George, John Maynard Keynes, Arthur Pigou, James Meade, E. F. Schumacher, Louis Kelso, Herman Daly, and James Lovelock. And special

Acknowledgments

thanks to James Boyce for years of friendship and intellectual collaboration.

Finally, as always, I am deeply grateful to my extended family: Zachary Barnes Miller, Eli Barnes, Leyna Bernstein, Pam Miller, Valerie Barnes Jordan, and Jess Almendarez.

Foreword

James K. Boyce

Ours introduces a transformative idea whose time is coming: universal property.

Universal property is a birthright belonging equally to all. It is individual, it is inalienable, and it is perfectly egalitarian. Unlike private property, universal property cannot be bought and sold, owned by corporations, or concentrated in a few hands. Unlike state property, income derived from the use of universal property flows not to governments but directly to the people themselves.

As Peter Barnes explains in this lucidly written book, universal property can help address some of the gravest failures in the functioning of markets and governments alike: above all, the growth of extreme inequalities of wealth and income and the destabilization of the Earth's climate by rampant carbon emissions. We urgently need innovative solutions that will reduce inequality without increasing carbon emissions, and reduce carbon emissions without increasing inequality.

In making the case for universal property, Barnes breaks from the well-worn state-versus-market divide that has delimited conventional political discourse in the past two centuries. He offers a fresh vision for the twenty-first century that draws on the pioneering works of earlier writers like Thomas Paine and Henry George, who also defied the ideological boxes that today we call "left" and "right."

At a time when inequality has metastasized – when twenty-five men in the world own more wealth than the bottom 4.5 billion – it is crucial that we create a more level playing field for all. Universal property is one way to move in this direction.

At a time when climate destabilization poses grave risks to millions of people here and now, and even graver risks to future generations, it is crucial to curtail the amount of fossil carbon we dump into the air, while at the same time protecting the real incomes of working families from increases in the prices of energy. Treating the limited capacity of the biosphere to absorb emissions as universal property is one way to do this.

At a time when many nations are sharply polarized along lines of race, ethnicity, class, and conflicting partisan loyalties, it is crucial to find shared interests and values that can help to unite us. Universal property is one way to build this common ground.

Offering a bold path to a more equitable, sustainable, and sane society, *Ours* will appeal to a readership as wide and diverse as the ownership of universal property itself.

Author's Note

Keep your eyes on the stars but your feet on the ground.

Theodore Roosevelt

Over the decades I've studied our economy from inside and out. As a journalist, I often wrote about it from the outside. Later, I co-founded businesses that probed the limits of capitalism from within. One was a worker-owned cooperative that installed solar heating systems in the 1970s. Another was a socially screened money-market fund called Working Assets, and a third was a progressive phone company called Credo Mobile.

In all these ventures, profit was a goal but not my primary one. My primary goal was to see whether, and by how much, businesses could shift, in a positive way, the behavior of our larger economy. Could they model good corporate behaviour that would then be emulated? Could they challenge the dominant algorithm of corporations, maximize return to shareholders? Could they non-trivially alter the flow of money through our economy?

Sadly, after twenty years, my conclusion was that, while socially minded companies can do good things, they can't change our economy by much; they are swimming against a tide that is too strong. What we need is not a few companies voluntarily behaving slightly better, but a system that makes *all* companies behave a lot better, whether intentionally or not. But how, very practically, could such a system be designed and installed?

More broadly, the need to repair or replace capitalism is now indisputable. This is not just because of the financial meltdown of 2008 or the Covid collapse of 2020. It is first and foremost because of markets' built-in systemic flaws — ever-widening inequality and disruption of nature. Those trajectories cannot continue. They must be turned in their opposite directions — toward greater equality and alignment with nature. But again, the practical question is *how*.

Ruminating on these questions, I came to the realization that something important is missing from markets. Modern humans are heirs to a vast trove of naturally and socially created wealth. This wealth legitimately belongs to all of us together and equally. It also comes with a duty to be preserved, if not enhanced, for future generations. The problem — and it's a huge one — is that this co-inherited cornucopia is simultaneously ignored, stolen, and destroyed by markets as structured today.

This is more than an intellectual failure; it is a real-world failure with vast social and planetary consequences. But the point of this book is that *it can be fixed*. If, through property rights, we recognize co-inherited wealth as assets to be preserved and beneficially owned by all persons equally, we could transform markets, societies, and our planet simultaneously. Instead of destroying nature, markets would protect it; instead of widening inequality, markets would reduce it. Yes, *markets* would do those things. And that would change everything.

With this realization in mind, I began putting together a mental model of an economy that retains the dynamism and efficiency of markets, but adds a new kind of property rights for large chunks of our co-inherited wealth. In this model, we would each inherit equal non-transferable shares of that co-inherited wealth and surrender them when we die. We would also co-inherit a legal obligation, administered by trustees, to preserve our joint inheritances for future generations. What I came to see was that this kind of property regime could, at scale, make markets work for everyone, including nature and future generations.

Let me make four quick points before you read on. First, the book will invite you to think differently about our economy than you probably have before. So be willing to take off your old economic glasses and put on a new pair.

Second, I've written the book for informed general readers, not experts. For that reason, I often skimp on details in order to keep the main argument clear. If you want more depth on a particular topic, the endnotes and bibliography can lead you to it.

Third, although the ideas expressed in this book can apply to all modern economies, they are a product of my experience in the United States, and are perhaps more applicable in Anglophone countries than elsewhere.

And finally, though I began writing this book long before

the Covid pandemic, the ideas expressed here are even more pertinent now than ever.

Peter Barnes
Point Reyes Station, California

What is Universal Property?

Capitalism as we know it has two egregious flaws: it relentlessly widens inequality and destroys nature. Its "invisible hand," which is supposed to transform individual self-seeking into widely shared well-being, too often doesn't, and governments can't keep up with the consequences. For billions of people around the world, the challenge of our era is to repair or replace capitalism before its cumulative harms become irreparable.

Among those who would repair capitalism, policy ideas abound. Typically, they involve more government regulations, taxes, and spending. Few, if any, would fundamentally alter the dynamics of markets themselves. Among those who would replace capitalism, many would nationalize a good deal of private property and expand government's role in regulating the rest.

This book explores the terrain midway between repairing and replacing capitalism. It envisions a hybrid market economy in which private property and businesses are complemented by universal property and fiduciary trusts, whose beneficiaries are future generations and all living persons equally.

Economists wrangle over monetary, fiscal, and regulatory

policies but pay little attention to property rights. Their models all assume that property rights remain just as they are forever. But this needn't and shouldn't be the case. My premise is that capitalism's most grievous flaws are, at root, problems of property rights and must be addressed at that level.

Property rights in modern economies are grants by governments of permission to use, lease, sell, or bequeath specific assets – and just as importantly, to exclude others from doing those things. The assets involved can be tangible, like land and machinery, or intangible, like shares of stock or songs.

Taken as a whole, property rights are akin to gravity: they curve economic space-time. Their tugs and repulsions are everywhere, and nothing can avoid them. And, just as water flows inexorably toward the ocean, so money, goods and power flow inexorably toward property rights. Governments can no more staunch these flows than King Canute could halt the tides.

That said, the most oft-forgotten fact about property rights is that they do not exist in nature; *they are constructs of human minds and societies*. The assets to which they apply may exist in nature, but the rights of humans to do things with them, or prevent others from doing them, do not. Their design and allocation are entirely up to us.

In this book, I take our existing fabric of property rights as both a given *and* merely the latest iteration in an evolutionary process that has been and will continue to be altered by living humans. Future iterations of the fabric will therefore be a product not only of the past, but also of our imagination and political will in the future. And, while eliminating existing property rights is difficult, adding new ones is less so.

Before we talk about universal property, we need to look at co-inherited wealth, for that is what universal property is based on.

A full inventory of co-inherited wealth would fill pages. Consider, for starters, air, water, topsoil, sunlight, fire, photosynthesis, seeds, electricity, minerals, fuels, cultivable plants, domesticable animals, law, sports, religion, calendars, recipes, mathematics, jazz, libraries, and the internet. Without these gifts and many more, our lives would be incalculably poorer.

Universal property does not involve all of those wonderful things. Rather, it focuses on a subset: the large, complex natural and social systems that support market economies, yet are excluded from representation in them. This subset includes natural ecosystems like the Earth's atmosphere and watersheds, and collective human constructs such as our legal, monetary and communications systems. All these systems are enormously valuable, in some cases priceless. Not only do our daily lives depend on them; they add prodigious value to markets, enabling corporations and private fortunes to grow to gargantuan sizes. Yet the systems were not built by anyone living today; they are all gifts we inherit together. So it is fair to ask, *who are their rightful beneficial owners?*

There are, essentially, three possibilities: no one, government, or all of us together equally. This book is about what happens if we choose the third option and create property rights to make it real.

Let's start with an obvious question: how much is this subset of co-inherited wealth worth? While it is impossible to put a precise number on this, estimates have been made. In 2000, the late Nobel economist Herbert Simon stated, "If we are very generous with ourselves, we might claim that we 'earned' as much as one fifth of [our present wealth]. The rest [eighty percent] is patrimony associated with being a member of an enormously productive social system, which has accumulated a vast store of physical capital and an even larger store of intellectual capital."[1]

Simon arrived at his estimate by comparing incomes in highly developed economies with those in earlier stages of development. The huge differences are due not to the rates of economic activity today – indeed, young economies often grow faster than mature ones – but to the much larger differences in institutions and know-how accumulated over decades. A few years later, World Bank economists William Easterly and Ross Levine confirmed Simon's math. They conducted a detailed study of rich and poor countries and asked what made them different. They found that it wasn't natural resources or the latest technologies. Rather, it was their social assets: the rule of law, property rights, a well-organized banking system, economic transparency, and a lack of corruption. All these collective assets played a far greater role than anything else.[2]

The preceding analysis doesn't include ecosystems gifted

to us by nature, but Robert Costanza and a worldwide team of scientists and economists took a crack at that in 1997. They found that natural ecosystems generate a global flow of benefits – including fresh water supply, soil formation, nutrient cycling, waste treatment, pollination, raw materials and climate regulation – worth between \$25 trillion and \$87 trillion a year.[3] That compares with a gross world product of about \$80 trillion.

These calculations suggest that we are greatly confused about where our wealth today comes from. We think it comes from the fevered efforts of today's businesses and workers, but in fact they merely add icing to a cake that was baked long ago.

The calculations also suggest that we should devote far more attention to co-inherited wealth than we currently do. Nowadays, economics textbooks don't even mention such wealth, much less its magnitude. Nor do Wall Street analysts or financial reporters. This is a grievous oversight that greatly

Figure 1 Where Today's Wealth Comes From

impedes our understanding of our economy. It is like trying to comprehend the universe without taking dark matter into account, or analyzing a business while ignoring over eighty percent of its assets.

Paying more attention to co-inherited wealth, however, is just a first step. If we want to change market outcomes, we need to *functionally connect* this wealth to real-time economic activity. And to do that, we need property rights, managers and beneficial owners.

What is it?

Universal property, as I use the term in this book, is a set of non-transferable rights backed by a subset of wealth we inherit together. Such property isn't mine, yours or the state's, but *ours* – literally held in trust for all of us, living and yet-to-be born. It belongs to us not because we earned it but because we co-inherited it, as if from common ancestors. This co-inheritance is, or should be, a universal economic right, just as voting is a universal political right.

To say that all of us are co-inheritors of universal property does not, however, mean that we should manage it ourselves, or that governments should. That job is best assigned to two types of institutions: trusts with a fiduciary responsibility to future generations, and social wealth funds that pay equal dividends to all living persons within their jurisdictions. An example of the latter is the Alaska Permanent Fund, which has paid equal dividends to every Alaskan since 1980. Examples of the former include large land trusts, such as the National Trust, a conserver of land and historic buildings in the UK, and thousands of local trusts, whose missions include land conservation, affordable housing, education, and community development.

An archetypal, albeit theoretical, example of universal property is the "sky trust" I proposed in my 2001 book, *Who Owns The Sky?* It is archetypal because it includes features of social wealth funds and fiduciary trusts simultaneously. In it, a fiduciary trust is charged with protecting the integrity of the atmosphere (or one nation's share of it) for future generations. It auctions a declining quantity of permits to bring burnable carbon into our economy, and divides the proceeds equally. A version of this model was introduced in Congress in 2009 by Representative (now Senator) Chris van Hollen of Maryland and re-introduced several times since.[4]

A bit of history may be useful here. For millennia, humans lived in tribes in which almost all property was communal. Individual land ownership emerged at the beginning of the Holocene when our ancestors became settled agriculturalists. Rulers granted ownership of land to heads of families, usually males. Often, military conquerors distributed land to their lieutenants. Titles could then be passed to heirs – typically, oldest sons got everything, a practice known as primogeniture. In Europe, Roman law codified these practices.

The Roman Institutes of Justinian distinguished three kinds of property:

- *res privatae*, private property owned by individuals, includ-ing land and personal items;
- *res publicae*, public property owned by the state, such as public buildings, aqueducts and roads; and
- *res communes*, common property, including air, water and shorelines.

The Institutes also identified a category called *res nullius*, or "nobody's things," that included uninhabited land and wild animals. Such things weren't immune to propertization; they just hadn't been propertized yet. Uninhabited land could be privatized by occupying it, wild animals by capturing them. A bird in hand was property; a bird in the bush was not.

In England during the Middle Ages, most of the valuable land was privately owned by barons, the Church and the Crown, but sizable common areas were also set aside for villagers. These commons were essential for the villagers' sustenance: they pro-vided food, water, firewood, building materials, and medicines.

There were many battles over what should be private and common. Until 1215, English kings granted exclusive fishing rights to their lieges; then, the Magna Carta established fisheries and forests as *res communes*. However, starting in the seven-teenth century and continuing into the nineteenth, in a process known as enclosure, local gentry fenced off village commons and converted them to private holdings. Impoverished peasants then drifted to cities and became industrial workers. Landlords invested their agricultural profits in manufacturing, and modern times, economically speaking, began.[5]

8

Universal property lies somewhere between individual and state property. In Roman terms, it converts a large swathe of *res nullius* into a species of *res communes:* instead of being owned by nobody, many gifts of nature and society would be owned beneficially by all.

While we are thinking historically, it is worth remembering that the limited liability corporation, which is so dominant today, is a relatively recent phenomenon. Prior to the nineteenth century, there were barely a handful of corporations in the UK and US; the dominant form of business organization was the partnership (in which all partners are liable for the partnership's debts). Limited liability corporations arose only when it became necessary to amass capital from strangers.

Similarly, until the eighteenth century, there was no such thing as intellectual property. Ideas and inventions floated freely in the air. The world's first copyright law, the Statute of Anne, was passed in England in 1710. Today, the world is flooded with copyrights, patents, trademarks, and trade secrets, all essential to the profits of giant corporations.

Like intellectual property, universal property can turn intangible assets into rights respected by markets and capable of generating income. And, like corporations that manage assets on behalf of shareholders, trusts can manage assets on behalf of future generations and all of us equally. The reason there is more intellectual than universal property today is that capital owners have fought for *their* most beneficial forms of property rights, while we, the people, haven't fought for ours. But that could change if we set our minds to it.

The idea of universal property isn't new. It was the invention of Thomas Paine, the English-born essayist who inspired America's revolution and much else. Indeed, virtually all the ideas in this book can be traced back to a single essay he wrote in the winter of 1795/96.

Paine led an extraordinary life. Unlike other American Founders, he wasn't born to privilege. The son of a Quaker corset-maker, he emigrated to Philadelphia in 1774 and found himself in the thick of pre-revolutionary ferment. Inspired, he wrote a pamphlet called *Common Sense,* which quickly sold half a million copies (in a nation of three million) and transformed the prevailing discontent with King George III into ardor for independence and a united democratic republic.

And that was just the beginning. Another series of essays, *The American Crisis*, kept the patriotic flame alive as the war for independence slogged. After America's victory, Paine returned to England to raise money for an iron bridge he wanted to build over the Schuylkill River in Philadelphia. While there, he wrote *Rights of Man* in response to Edmund Burke's repudiation of the French Revolution. Charged with sedition, he escaped to France, where he was greeted as a hero and elected to the National Assembly. Then came the Jacobin Terror, during which he was sentenced to death for having opposed the execution of Louis XVI. He spent ten months in Luxembourg Prison before being saved by the American ambassador, James Monroe, who persuaded his captors that Paine was a citizen of the United States, France's ally, not Britain, its foe.

It was during his years in France that Paine wrote his last

great essay, *Agrarian Justice*. In *Rights of Man*, Paine had criticized the English Poor Laws and argued for what today would be called a welfare state, including universal education, pensions for the elderly and employment for the urban poor, all paid for by taxes. In *Agrarian Justice* he went farther, arguing that poverty should be systemically eliminated with universal income from jointly inherited property.[6]

There are two kinds of property, he wrote: "firstly, property that comes to us from the Creator of the universe – such as the Earth, air and water; and secondly, artificial or acquired property – the invention of men." Because humans have different talents and luck, the latter kind of property must necessarily be distributed unequally, but the first kind belongs to everyone equally. It is the "legitimate birthright" of every man and woman.

To Paine, this was more than an abstract idea; it was something that could be implemented within a *laissez faire* economy. But how? How could the Earth, air and water possibly be distributed equally to everyone? Paine's practical answer was that, though the assets themselves can't be distributed equally, income derived from them can be.

How again? Here Paine came up with an ingenious solution. He proposed a "national fund" to pay every man and woman about $18,000 (in today's dollars) at age twenty-one, and $12,000 a year after age fifty-five. In effect, nature's gifts would be transformed into grants and annuities that would give every young person a start in life and every older person a dignified retirement. Revenue would come from "ground rent" paid by private landowners upon their deaths. Paine used contemporary French and English data to show that a ten percent inheritance tax – his mechanism for collecting ground rent – could fully pay for the universal grants and annuities.

An important nuance here is that the rent would be collected not only on a deceased person's land, but on his entire estate. It would thereby recoup many of society's gifts as well as nature's. And in Paine's view, there was nothing wrong with this. "Separate an individual from society, and give him an island or a continent to possess, and he cannot ... be rich. All accumulation therefore of personal property, beyond what a man's own hands produce, is derived to him by living in society; and he owes, on every principle of justice, of gratitude, and of civilization, a part of that accumulation back again to society from whence the whole came."

What Paine invented here, in my retrospective opinion, was a prescient stroke of genius. Long before Wall Street sliced collateralized debt obligations into risk-based tranches, Paine designed a simple way to monetize co-inherited wealth for the equal benefit of everyone. It is a model as relevant – and revolutionary – today as it was then.

Why Markets Fail

The reason we need universal property is that, without it, markets fail in calamitous ways. Let us see how and why.

At first glance, markets are amazing things. They spur people to work, generate prodigious wealth, and once their basic rules are established, largely take care of themselves. That's because markets do two things really well: process vast amounts of information in real time, condensing it into simple numbers called prices; and reflect a kind of "general will," as in *this is what the market thinks*.

But that superficial view is deceiving. What markets think is not, in fact, what *everybody* thinks. Markets represent the general will of those with money today, and no one else. No money today means no voice, no vote and no power in markets. It should therefore come as no surprise that, even in the world's most productive economies, people sleep in the streets, die of preventable diseases and suffer constant economic anxiety. Nor should it astonish that nature and future generations, with no money at all, get no respect in markets whatsoever.

Economists use the term *market failure* to describe situations in which, as textbook author N. Gregory Mankiw puts it, "the market on its own fails to allocate resources efficiently." Classic examples include excess profits extracted by monopolies and harms caused by pollution.[1]

This is a reasonable definition of market failure if efficient allocation of scarce resources is our primary concern. If, however, we have larger goals, such as a stable society and a liveable planet, market failure is something else. It is the failure to advance these larger goals *at all*, whether efficiently or not – or worse, to efficiently advance their opposites. So I will continue to use the term *market failure*, but with the caveat that the failure must be measured against the *meta* goals of our economy.

Let me expand on that last phrase. *Micro*-economics focuses on the behaviors of households and firms and how supply and demand affect prices and vice-versa. *Macro*-economics focuses on the relationships between aggregate phenomena such as employment, interest rates, inflation and the *summum bonum*, gross domestic product (GDP). In the 1970s, British economist E. F. Schumacher introduced the concept of "*meta*-economics" as a step beyond macro. Its focus would be on the relationships between our monetized economy and the larger realms of nature, society, and the human psyche. And its goal would be to make those relationships as stable and mutually beneficial as possible.[2]

Schumacher's goal can be described in other ways. We could say that markets should aim for the most well-being for the most people while staying within the thresholds of nature. Or we could use the visual metaphor proffered by British economist Kate Raworth, who compares our ideal economy to a doughnut bounded by an ecological ceiling and a social floor.

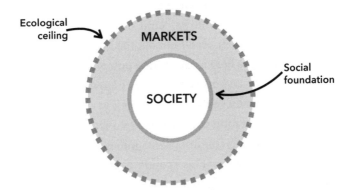

Figure 2 Raworth's Doughnut

Our paramount goal, she says, must be to get markets inside the doughnut's boundaries and keep them there.[3]

The three market failures

With the preceding considerations in mind, let's now look at the market's three biggest failures: ever-widening inequality, disruption of nature, and a third slightly lesser failing, financial instability. What lies behind them, and how might they be fixed?

Market failure #1: ever-widening inequality
As Marriner Eccles, chair of the Federal Reserve from 1934 to 1948, wrote about the Great Depression, "A giant suction pump had by 1929–30 drawn into a few hands an increasing

portion of currently produced wealth ... In consequence, as in a poker game where the chips are concentrated in fewer and fewer hands, the other fellows could stay in the game only by borrowing. When their credit ran out the game stopped."[4]

What interests us here is the suction pump. (We'll come back to the poker game and borrowing later.) How does the suction pump work, and why can't we constrain it?

Wealth concentration is a repetitive two-step dance. It begins with unequal starting conditions, magnifies those initial differences, and then repeats. This is aptly captured by the Biblical algorithm, "To them that hath, more shall be given."[5]

Most people know this instinctively. They know that money begets money and that, relatively speaking, the rich get richer while the poor get poorer. They see how the rich use their initial advantages – money, education, connections – to gain even more advantages. And they sense, accurately, that money has the loudest voice in politics.

But what lies beneath the dance? *Why* does wealth endlessly concentrate? Part of the answer is that property commands more market power than labor. While wage earners are paid only for their own efforts, property owners gain from many people's efforts. Further, while wage earners are paid only for current efforts, property owners reap from past, present, and even future efforts (because stock markets capitalize expected future income into current prices). What's more, since collateral is needed to borrow money, only those who already own property can use other people's money to acquire more.

The inherent advantages of property, plus its historically

unequal distribution, combine to produce the result that French economist Thomas Piketty summed up mathematically as $r > g$: the return to capital exceeds the growth rate of the economy as a whole. Which means that capital owners continuously extract money from elsewhere in the economy. *That* is Eccles' suction pump.

From whom or where does capital extract that money? Marx believed it comes from workers, which is true but only part of the story. To an even greater degree, capital extracts financial value from our co-inherited wealth (mostly in the form of higher share prices) while paying almost nothing for it.

Consider, for example, Mark Zuckerberg, the founder and largest shareholder of Facebook. According to *Forbes* magazine, Zuckerberg is the fourth richest person in the world, with a net worth exceeding $90 billion.[6] No one doubts that he is brilliant and hardworking, but there is no conceivable way any mortal can earn $90 billion in ten years. The reason Zuckerberg is so wealthy is that the value of Facebook's stock comes overwhelmingly from co-inherited wealth: the internet, computers, silicon chips, and all the science and research that preceded them, not to mention the millions of people whose eyeballs supply its revenue base. Though Zuckerberg himself might not acknowledge this, his fellow billionaire Warren Buffett has been frank: "I personally think that society is responsible for a very significant portion of what I've earned."[7]

Market failure #2: disruption of nature

As many of us recall from school, the Earth has passed through numerous geological ages: Cenozoic, Jurassic, Cambrian, and so on. All sorts of dramatic things happened in those early ages. Continents drifted, volcanoes erupted, asteroids crashed, glaciers moved, oceans rose and fell, species appeared and vanished. All these commotions were caused by natural forces. Humans played no role at all.

Scientists call the age we live in now the Holocene. It began some twelve thousand years ago when the last Ice Age ended. Since then the Earth has remained remarkably calm and congenial to life. We humans took advantage of this congeniality to develop agriculture, cities, and iPhones. But while we did these things, we also razed forests, dammed rivers, fouled the air, filled the land with chemicals, and depleted the oceans of fish. The result is that the majority of ecosystems on Earth are now shaped by humans, and non-human species are vanishing about 1,000 times faster than in the early Holocene.

This planetary reshaping is what Paul Crutzen, a Nobel chemist, was pondering during a scientific conference in 2001. When one of the speakers used the word "Holocene," Crutzen turned to a colleague and whispered, "No, damn it, we are in the Anthropocene," inventing the word on the fly (*anthropo* means *human* in Greek). Since Crutzen's epiphany and subsequent scholarly article, the term has been widely used by scientists and is being considered by the International Commission on Stratigraphy, the body that adopts the official names of geological eras.[8]

The basic idea of the Anthropocene is that *Homo sapiens* is no run-of-the-mill species; it is a geological force, like plate tectonics. We have the power to reshape the entire planet and eradicate millions of non-human species, and are currently doing so. We've built an economic juggernaut that is like a runaway bulldozer. We can't go on like this, a rational person would think, and yet we do – for a couple of reasons.

One is the dominance of profit-maximizing corporations. These powerful entities are non-stop growth machines. Each year they must sell more than the year before. If they don't, their value deflates and their managers are eventually sacked.

A second reason is that nature and markets don't talk with each other. The biosphere communicates with chemicals while markets talk with money. There is no *lingua franca*. It does no good, for example, for a CEO to learn that the concentration of carbon dioxide in our atmosphere has risen fifty percent since 1750 and that future generations will suffer mightily because of this. What the CEO needs to know is how that will affect her bottom line this year. Chemical information doesn't tell her that; prices would.

Harms caused to nature and society are the shadow side of human economic activity. In warfare such harms are called collateral damage; in economics they are called *negative externalities*. (There are *positive* externalities too, as when one person's home improvements enhance their neighbors' property values, but we'll ignore those here.)

The first major economist to take negative externalities seriously was Arthur Pigou, a colleague of John Maynard Keynes at Cambridge. His greatest work, *The Economics of Welfare*, wasn't nearly as influential as Keynes' *General Theory of Employment, Interest and Money*, but re-reading it today affords many valuable insights.

When *The Economics of Welfare* was published in 1920, "welfare" meant human well-being in its broadest sense, not government money transfers as we use the term today. Pigou believed that the primary goal of an economy was to create the most welfare for the most people. Central to his thinking was the notion that markets produce bads as well as goods, disservices as well as services, *illth* (to use John Ruskin's apt word) as well as wealth. Welfare is therefore not the *sum* of goods and services produced, as most economists think today, but rather the *difference* between that sum and the harms the economy also produces. Both sides of the ledger matter. Well-being can be increased by reducing harms as well as by adding goods.

The detractors from well-being that Pigou worried most about were poverty and pollution. His calculus on poverty was simple: "any transference of income from a relatively rich man to a relatively poor man of similar temperament, since it enables more intense wants, must increase the aggregate sum of satisfaction."[9]

Pigou is most remembered, however, for his thinking about pollution. In his era the most notable form this took was coal smoke in cities. Pigou wanted to reduce this smoke and thereby increase the well-being of city dwellers. But how? His big idea was for governments to tax sales of coal. Harms caused by coal would then diminish, and as a bonus, governments would reap more revenue.

A century later, the world is lightly peppered with Pigovian taxes on pollution, alcohol, tobacco, congestion, plastic bags, and sugary drinks. But have they worked? To a degree, yes, but especially with regard to pollution, not nearly well enough. Governments have been reluctant to tax pollution steeply for two reasons: polluting companies don't like steep taxes because they reduce profits; and ordinary citizens don't like them either because they raise prices of daily essentials. Hence, a century after Pigou's *magnum opus*, coal burning has metastasized into the market failure that is eating the planet. The lesson I draw from this is that Pigovian taxes by themselves are insufficient to prevent severe harms to nature. Something more is needed.

Market failure #3: Financial instability

All complex systems have ebbs and flows, and markets are no exception. Business cycles can't be eliminated; they can only be tempered and cushioned. Bubbles and crashes, however, aren't business cycles; they are systemic breakdowns caused by too much speculation and debt. While such breakdowns aren't quite as iniquitous as wealth concentration and disruption of nature, they are repetitive and painful, and something needs to be done about them.

In writing about the 1929 crash, Eccles cited three causes: an upward money pump, a poker game (i.e. speculation) and debt. Earlier we looked at the suction pump; now let's look at speculation and debt.

There is a crucial difference between entrepreneurial risk-taking and financial speculation. The former drives innovation and growth; the latter mostly drives more speculation – and ultimately, bubbles and crashes. An ideal economic system would encourage the former and discourage the latter. At the moment, ours does the opposite.

In a poker game, to use Eccles' metaphor, there are winners and losers, but no increase in total wealth. The same is true for almost all the betting Wall Street promotes.

As for debt, its most useful function is to shift economic activity forward in time. If all new production and consumption had to be paid for by savings from the past, economic activity would be much slower than it is now. Debt enables us to make and buy things today and pay for them later. If used judiciously, it is a helpful tool.

The challenge with debt is to use it productively rather than speculatively. Debt is tempting to speculators because it can multiply their winnings exponentially. Consider a simple mortgage. If you pay cash for a $100,000 house and sell it later for $200,000, you will have doubled your original investment. By contrast, if you put $10,000 down, borrow $90,000 and sell the house for the same $200,000, you will have earned *eleven* times your original investment ($110,000 on a $10,000 investment), minus some interest. This is what speculators call *leverage*.

The trouble with leverage is that it duct-tapes together a financial house of cards that sooner or later will collapse. This process was diagnosed several decades ago by Hyman Minsky, a little-known economist who died in 1996. He observed that debt grows in three stages. The first, when debt is fully repayable by cash flow, is stable. The second, when borrowers use cash flow to pay interest but roll the principal into new loans, is stable as long as the economy is humming. The third, which Minsky called "Ponzi financing," is when cash flow covers neither interest nor principal. When that stage arrives, the house of cards is ready to tumble.[10]

The systemic nature of the problem lies in the fact that one stage leads inexorably to the next. Minsky's conclusion was that, because of excessive speculative debt, *good times automatically breed instability*. Unless speculative debt is curbed, prosperity creates its own undoing. In 2009, Nobel economist Paul Krugman acknowledged that "we are all Minskyites now."

Another way to view market failures is through the lens of complex systems. Briefly, a complex system is a conglomeration of many moving parts that continuously interact. Such systems exist everywhere in the universe, from the atomic level to the galactic, and they exhibit a number of similar behaviors.

In recent decades, the study of complex systems has emerged as a new frontier in many disciplines, including economics. Among its findings are that complex systems are highly sensitive to initial conditions, path dependent (meaning that what happens in the future builds on what happened in the past), and subject to dramatic phase changes that can't be predicted.[11]

What is most relevant here is how complex systems self-regulate. The keys are *homeostasis* and *feedback*. Homeostasis, from the Greek words for "same" and "steady," is the ability of complex systems to stabilize themselves in response to external changes. The classic example is the ability of warm-blooded animals to maintain a steady internal temperature amid fluctuations in ambient temperature. Something similar occurs in trees, which regulate their leaf temperature through evapo-transpiration.

Underlying homeostasis is a mechanism called feedback. Feedback is what happens when an organism, machine, or system receives information from its surroundings and changes its behavior in response. It operates in two directions. One, called negative, works to dampen the system's behavior – for example, if it's too hot, the system cools itself. The other, called positive, amplifies the initial behavior. Negative feedback keeps a complex system in balance while positive feedback gives it forward momentum. But too much positive feedback – or too little of the negative kind – can tip it toward collapse.

A good example of negative feedback is the governor invented in 1788 by James Watt to control the speed of his steam engine. As the engine speeds up, centrifugal force lifts two fly-balls on hinged arms, which causes a valve to narrow the air inlet, slowing the engine down. More complex examples are the immune systems of living organisms, in which antibodies identify and dispose of foreign agents.

An example of positive feedback is what happens when an open microphone is within range of a loud speaker. Sound from the speaker flows into the microphone, out of the speaker again, and so on, until the noise becomes unbearable. An economic example is what happens during a speculative bubble. When

Charles Prince, the CEO of Citigroup in 2008, was asked why his bank continued to package subprime loans, even when it knew they were risky, his answer was, "As long as the music is playing, you've got to get up and dance."[12]

Though the three market failures vary in detail, they share two similarities. One is that all are *failures of homeostasis*. In each case, markets have sped down a road too far or too fast and been unable to restrain themselves before excessive harms have occurred. Just as financial speculation creates its own undoing, so do wealth concentration and disruption of nature.

The second similarity is that all are *failures of omission*. Imagine an automobile with no steering wheel or brakes. There might be nothing wrong with any of its active parts, but if let loose on a highway it will surely run into trouble. Its problem is that crucial pieces are missing. Just as every car needs a steering wheel and brakes, and every democracy needs checks and balances, so every economy needs countervailing forces and self-correcting mechanisms.

To put this another way, markets fail to achieve their meta goals because they lack braking and balancing agents. Only living individuals, corporations, labor unions and the state have any sway in real-time markets. Nature, future generations and all members of society *as a whole* have no agents at all. But there's no reason that can't change.

3

Twenty-First-Century Realities

When complex systems fail, it is usually because their internal gearings are out of synch with their external surroundings, which change over time. In the last chapter we looked at markets' inner failures; here we look at the outward realities with which they must align.

The twenty-first century will be – indeed, already is – vastly different from previous eras. Markets and governments are flailing, social divisions are mounting, and our planet is entering a tumultuous geological transition. It is clear we must act in fundamentally new ways, but how?

To address that question, we need a new set of economic eye glasses. It is hard to chart a path forward when our vision is clouded with ideas that took hold decades ago.

For example, mainstream economics would have us believe that:

- When markets grow, a rising tide lifts all boats;
- Harms caused by market activity can be adequately regulated and/or mitigated by government;
- Financial institutions invest people's savings productively.

Such notions are obsolete. Today's realities are:

- When markets grow, the rising tide lifts mostly yachts.
- The accumulation of harms to nature caused by insufficiently constrained markets is why the Holocene is history.
- Financial institutions allocate more money to speculation than to creation of real wealth.

Why do so many economists cling to their outdated beliefs? It may help to see the mental model on which their beliefs are based. Almost every economics textbook begins with a picture like Figure 3.

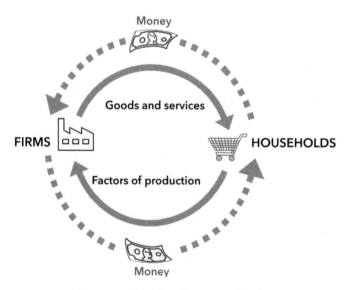

Figure 3 How Our Economy Works

In this idealized economy, identical households supply factors of production (labor and capital, mostly) to same-sized competing firms who use them to produce goods and services. Households pay firms for the goods and services, and firms pay households for the factors of production. Thus, production inputs, goods, and services circulate in one direction while money circulates in the other. Fortuitously, the total of what firms produce roughly equals what households consume. In theory, everything is in equilibrium and the circles can spin around forever.

What's wrong with this picture? An astonishing amount. Let's begin with the assumption that our economy exists in a void. A more accurate picture would show it as a subset of two larger systems, human society and the biosphere. It cannot be stated often enough that our economy is entirely dependent on these host systems and must, at a minimum, avoid destabilizing them. Yet the host systems show up neither in economists' models nor in the machinery of markets themselves.

Then there is the implication, or at least the simplification, that all households and firms are identical. Of course, economists don't really believe this; they *assume* it because it makes their computations easier. But while convenient, the simplification fixates their attention on aggregate sums rather than the divergences within them.

The reality, of course, is that firms and households are far from equal. A small minority of wealthy firms and households out-punches all the others. This is so for two reasons: unequal starting conditions, and a playing field tilted toward previously accumulated wealth.

Or ponder the presumed circular flow of money from households to firms and back again. Nowadays, most of the money in circulation *doesn't* pass through households and firms and *isn't* used for wages or productive investment. Instead, it is siphoned into a speculative casino of stocks, bonds, and derivatives, a diversion found nowhere in the conventional model.

At this point we are ready to dive into twenty-first-century economic reality. A good place to start is with a reconsideration of scarcity. Making the best use of scarce resources is what markets are supposed to be about. But what is a "scarce resource" or "best use" can and *should* change over time.

For most of human existence, we survived on what we hunted and gathered. As agriculture and fixed settlements arose, so did specialization of labor, trading, and a higher standard of living. All of this accelerated rapidly after capitalism and industrialization took off in the eighteenth century.

Sometime around 1950, capitalism entered a new phase. In 1958, John Kenneth Galbraith wrote a best-seller called *The Affluent Society*, in which he argued that scarcity of goods was now a thing of the past, at least in advanced economies. "So great has been the change that many of the desires of the individual are no longer even evident to him. They become so only as they are synthesized, elaborated, and nurtured by advertising and salesmanship."[1]

Though it wasn't recognized at the time, this was a major

phase change for capitalism. Before it, people wanted – in fact, *needed* – more goods than markets produced. Demand, in other words, exceeded supply. After the change, we shifted into surplus mode. Now, there is no limit to what firms can produce; their problem is finding households to buy it. A sizable chunk of GDP is spent persuading people to buy what Dr. Seuss, in *The Lorax*, aptly called *thneeds*.[2] And credit is lavishly extended so people can pay for them.

When shortage economies become surplus economies, many things change. For one thing, the law of diminishing returns kicks in and more "stuff" produces less happiness. For another, while scarcities still exist, their nature is qualitatively different. In shortage times, the chief scarcity was goods. Today, there remains a lack of goods for some, but it isn't due to a lack of productive capacity – it is due to people's inability to pay. The critical scarcity, in other words, isn't goods but income.

Similarly, in the early capitalist era, land, resources, and places to dump wastes were abundant, while financial capital was scarce. That's why property rights and institutions (e.g. limited liability corporations and tradable shares of stock) were developed that put capital above all else. Today, we are awash in financial capital and literally running out of nature. Which suggests it is time for property rights that put nature's interests first.

Then there is the matter of time. For millennia, human labor was unpaid and seasonal; today it is the basis for hourly and monthly wages. In the nineteenth century it was not unusual for people to work twelve-hour days, six days a week; in the

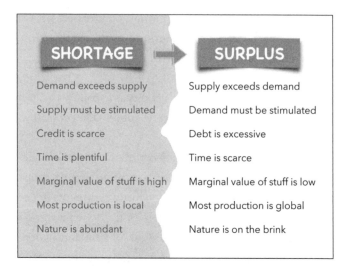

Figure 4 Phases of Market Development

twentieth, thanks to trade union pressure, eight-hour days and five-day work weeks became the norm. But in the US since 1970, despite a ten-fold increase in output per capita, we've been working harder than ever to make ends meet. More often than not, it takes multiple jobs and breadwinners to support a family. Parents lack time for their children, and everyone lacks time to relax and enjoy non-remunerative pursuits. For countless numbers of people, life is rushed, precarious, stressful, and unfulfilling.

These twenty-first-century realities lead to the conclusion that our definition of "scarce resources" is overdue for an update. Higher on our scarcity list than goods, I'd argue, should be household income, nature, and time outside the labor market. These scarcities can be partially addressed with taxes and regulations, but if we want markets to address them too, we need to embed them in our fabric of property rights.

Another way to sniff out today's reality is to follow the money. This means observing how money enters our economy and how it flows thereafter.

The first fact to absorb is that, contrary to common understanding, only a minuscule percentage of circulating money is printed, minted, or otherwise created by governments or central banks. Almost all of it is created electronically by private banks that lend it into existence. As the Bank of England matter-of-factly explains, "banks do not act simply as intermediaries, lending out deposits that savers place with them. Rather, whenever a bank makes a loan, it simultaneously creates a matching deposit in the borrower's bank account, thereby creating new money."[3]

In theory, banks direct this newly created money into productive undertakings, but that isn't what banks actually do these days. As Rana Foroohar, a reporter at *Time* and CNN, put it in her book *Makers and Takers*, "Today finance engages mostly in alchemy, issuing massive amounts of debt and funneling money to different parts of the financial system itself."[4]

If sentient Martians were to land on Earth today, they would observe not one but two human economies: one for producing goods and services, the other for betting on the future value of existing assets. The first of these – our real economy – is the one we live in every day. In it, products are made and sold, and money flows back and forth between households and firms. The sum of all goods and services sold – gross domestic product – is a reasonable, if not perfect, measure of this economy.

The second economy, which can be likened to a casino, produces nothing and is therefore excluded from GDP, so its size isn't measured by the government. There is, however, a way to gauge its magnitude. The starting point is Fedwire, a clearing house operated by the Federal Reserve through which US financial institutions electronically transfer funds to each other. Every dollar that changes hands in the US (except in cash or crypto-currencies) passes through Fedwire or two smaller clearing houses. In 2019, the clearing houses handled nearly $1 *quadrillion* in monetary transactions.[5] By contrast, the total of all goods and services sold that year came to a mere $21 trillion,

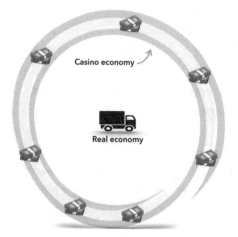

Figure 5 The Two Economies

or two percent of monetary transactions. These numbers suggest that the casino economy, in monetary terms, is roughly *fifty times* bigger than our real economy.

What does the bloated casino do for our real economy? On the positive side, it provides liquidity for exiting entrepreneurs, shuffles risk to those most willing to bear it, and allows banks to manage their reserves efficiently. On the negative side, it sucks more money out of the real economy than it puts in, serves as a round-the-clock enforcer of profit maximization, and is the place where concentrated wealth grows while being passed from one generation to the next.

These negative effects could perhaps be tolerated if the casino were small, but, as we've noted, it isn't. As John Maynard Keynes put it, "Speculators may do no harm as bubbles on a steady stream of enterprise, but the situation is serious when enterprise becomes the bubble on a whirlpool of speculation."[6]

In short, the size, complexity, and fragility of our monetary casino add huge systemic risk to our real economy. It isn't enough, therefore, to regulate the casino; we also have to shrink it and channel much of its money and human energy into real goods and services.

This brings us back to the most critical scarcity (nature aside) in our economy today: household income. The primary reason household income is scarce is that most of it comes from labor, and labor is losing its never-ending battle with capital for income share.

Recall that households get their incomes by selling factors

of production to firms. Starting with Adam Smith, economists identified three factors of production that households own: land (including natural resources), labor, and capital. More recently they've added entrepreneurship. All are essential for the production of goods and services, and all get paid what markets will bear. Landowners collect rent, laborers earn wages, capital owners get interest and dividends, and entrepreneurs, when successful, reap large capital gains.

From the standpoint of households, the problem is that, in order to get income from a factor of production, you have to own it. And while every adult (barring slaves and prisoners) owns the right to their labor, ownership of land and capital is highly concentrated and, in many cases, inherited. This wouldn't matter if labor commanded, say, three quarters of factor income, but that isn't the case. Capital owners always seek to cut labor costs, and they've done so brilliantly over the last fifty years thanks to automation, globalization, the growth of finance, and the suppression of labor unions. As a result, labor's share of personal income has steadily declined over the last fifty years, while capital's has risen.[7]

In the twenty-first century, the inconvenient truth is that *labor income by itself can no longer sustain a large middle class.* That twentieth-century dream is now a chimera. If we want a large middle class in this century, and all that goes with it (including democracy), we *must* supplement labor income with non-labor income. That doesn't mean we shouldn't fight for higher wages. It means we should fight for higher wages *and* broader flows of non-labor income. Both are essential.

This is where universal property comes in. Remember that there's a major factor of production that economists and markets largely ignore: the natural and social systems that are part of our co-inherited wealth. And therein lies a potential bonanza. In a purely financial sense, that sizable chunk of our co-inheritance can be seen as both an under-compensated factor of production and a potential source of income to its rightful beneficiaries. And these untapped potentials are linked. If our co-inherited systems *charged* for the value they add to the real and casino economies, as all other production factors do, and then divided the revenues equally among their rightful owners, a sizable stream of new income would flow to all of us.

Universal property, properly structured, can therefore play two critical roles in markets. It can make markets heed future generations, and as a result, nature; and it can convert chunks of our co-inherited wealth into lifelong income for everyone. Best of all, once set up, it can do those things largely on its own, as long as civil law prevails.

4

The Jobs of Universal Property

About twenty years ago, I co-authored a report called *The State of The Commons*, patterned after corporate reports to shareholders. The report quoted former US Secretary of the Interior Walter Hickel, a Republican, who said, "If you steal $10 from a man's wallet, you are likely to get into a fight. But if you steal billions from the commons, co-owned by him and his descendants, he may not even notice." The report concluded that "our shared inheritance is being grossly mismanaged. Maintenance is terrible, theft is rampant and rents often aren't being collected. To put it bluntly, our common wealth – and our children's – is being squandered."[1]

The most immediate job of universal property, then, is to halt the squandering of co-inherited wealth. It can do that by cloaking co-inheritances with the sorts of property rights used to protect private wealth, with the important proviso that the beneficiaries of universal property rights are, by definition, universal.

The meta-economic job for universal property goes further: it is to keep markets from destroying our social fabric and our planet – or to put it more positively, to make markets work as we need them to. *How* to do this is the meta-economic question at hand. Schumacher suggested that markets include "goods" that, in some way, represent the "irreplaceable capital" of nature and society. Universal property is a way we can do that and more.[2]

How universal property would work

It is time to take a deeper look at the components of universal property and how they might work together.

Trusts

If corporations are the ideal agents for maximizing short-term profit, trusts are the optimal agents for preserving assets in perpetuity. Like corporations, they are self-governing, potentially immortal fictitious entities that can own and manage property for as long as they pay their bills and taxes. Also like corporations, they have governing boards that are accountable to their beneficial owners. Where trusts and corporations differ is in who their beneficial owners are and what their governing boards are obliged to do.

Trusts were invented in twelfth-century England to protect owners of estates who went off to the Crusades and wanted to get their lands back when they returned. The trust arrangement created a useful distinction between a beneficial owner of property and a trustee, who must always serve the beneficial owner. That was and remains the best solution humans have yet devised to assure that managers of other people's property stay loyal to those they serve.

At the heart of trusts is the concept of *fiduciary duty*: a person who manages assets for other people owes one hundred percent loyalty to those people. It is similar to the duty lawyers owe to their clients. As US Supreme Court Justice Benjamin Cardozo once put it, "Not honesty alone, but the punctilio of an honor the most sensitive, is the standard of behavior" for a fiduciary.[3]

It is important to note that a trustee's duties are different from those of an elected official. Politicians in a democracy are open to influence from all quarters – and so they should be. Fiduciaries, by contrast, may listen to many points of view but must always act out of undivided loyalty to their beneficiaries.

What universal property does is to subject some of our co-inherited wealth to fiduciary rules, rather than profit-maximizing or political ones. This may at first seem undemo-cratic, but neither markets nor representative democracies have been ideal guardians for those who can't vote, speak, or spend money. Indeed, a good case can be made that universal prop-erty *expands* democracy – at least when it comes to manage-ment of co-inherited wealth – by including proxies for future generations and nature. There may be irony in the thought that fictitious entities developed to protect English barons can also protect ecosystems and democratic societies, but if the entities work, why not use them?

Universal beneficiaries

Beneficiaries of trusts are passive rather than active owners; they receive the benefits of their property without having to manage it. Thus, private trusts are often established to ben-efit children and grandchildren, while charitable trusts are established to benefit hospitals, universities, and the like. Often, the trusts function as endowments that enable institutions to receive income in perpetuity.

A distinguishing feature of universal property trusts is that they have *universal* beneficiaries – i.e. all living and future persons within a specified jurisdiction. No legal resident is excluded, and all are treated equally. Becoming a beneficiary is a non-transferable birthright that expires at death. Persons born outside the jurisdiction can register under residency rules, and need not be "citizens" in the political sense.

It is important to note that the set of universal beneficiaries includes two subsets: future generations and all people living today. The interests of these subsets will often align, but not always. In cases of non-alignment, the interests of future generations come first. *Preservation of co-inheritances* is the highest priority for universal property trusts. Only if income is generated while an asset is being preserved – for example, if fees are charged for use of the asset – can it be distributed to living persons. In such cases, the default distribution formula is one person, one share.

Birthrights

Right now, no child has a legally established right to begin life with an inheritance. About one in four Americans receives *some* money from a parent or grandparent, though often not until late in life. And not surprisingly, these private inheritances are grossly unequal: the wealthiest one percent gets more than everyone else combined.[4]

One of the most important benefits of universal property is that it makes *every* baby a trust-fund baby. It does this by conveying two sorts of inheritances equally to everyone: natural and social assets held in permanent trust, and a monetized endowment that can provide lifelong income to everyone. Along with the inheritances, however, comes a duty of care. It is a fair deal: we, the living, get income now, and in return must assure that future generations don't lose *their* birthrights.

Usage and non-usage rights

As every law student knows, property rights aren't one thing, they are a bundle of rights. This bundle includes the rights to possess, sell, lease, use, enjoy, encumber, and/or gift a tangible or intangible asset – and just as importantly, to exclude others from doing those things. Furthermore, these rights can be sliced and diced almost any which way.

Within this passel of possibilities, universal property focuses on rights to use, lease, and exclude others from using co-inherited assets. In practical terms, this means rights to limit and charge for transient use. One of the cardinal flaws of markets today is that they *don't* charge for transient use of co-inherited assets, but they could and should.

A *covenant* or *easement* is a right to use a property that someone else owns – typically, to walk or drive across it. A *restrictive covenant* or *conservation easement* is the reverse of that – an agreement that *prevents* specified uses of an asset that someone else owns. Such covenants were used for decades in the United States to bar African-Americans from private housing, until the Supreme Court held such discrimination unconstitutional in 1948. More positively, conservation easements can be excellent tools for preserving gifts of nature or history without owning the underlying land. They can potentially be used not only to protect specific pieces of land, but entire ecosystems as well.

What about government?

The case for transforming markets with universal property must confront an obvious question: why not just use government to regulate and tax? My answer has two parts. One has to do with the limits of government, the other with the advantages of universal property.

First, as the unremitting crises of climate change and inequality remind us daily, government has more than met its match in profit-maximizing corporations. Yes, it has the authority to regulate and tax those corporations, but its will to do so is severely circumscribed by the corporations' unlimited use of money, media, and lobbying. Time after time, legislatures and agencies have been captured by industries they are supposed to regulate. If occasionally an effective regulation slips through, it is often whittled down later when political winds shift. And this problem isn't easily fixed; it is what happens when winner-take-all capitalism inhabits a pliable democracy.

On the other side of the coin, universally owned property rights have several advantages over government when it comes to altering market outcomes. One is durability. Politicians and policies come and go, but property rights endure. Once created, they can't easily be taken away. Universal property is thus more likely than regulations or taxes to withstand the slings and arrows of well-funded opponents.

Another advantage of universal property is fiduciary duty. Politicians are legally bound only to support the Constitution; after that they can favor any interest groups they want. By contrast, trustees of universal property are bound by law to serve only future generations and all living persons equally. If trustees deviate from their fiduciary duty, they can be sued, fined, or removed.

A final advantage of universal property is its direct link to everyone's bank accounts and hence daily lives. That is not the case with most government policies. Because of this cash nexus, people will pay attention to their universal property and defend it politically. Just ask any Alaska politician.

I am not ideologically opposed to government any more than I am ideologically opposed to markets. To the contrary, I believe there are things government *should* be doing that it isn't. That said, more universal property would make government's work a lot easier. If markets protected nature better, government would have fewer harms to clean up; if they distributed income more equitably, government would have less stress and misery to remediate. From this perspective, universal property isn't a substitute for government, but a very useful ally.

A tour of the territory

Universal property at this time is mostly an idea, but there are numerous prototypes we can learn from. The examples that follow are meant to be suggestive rather than definitive. No single example contains every feature described above, but every feature is represented somewhere. Also included are proposals that are similar to universal property but lack one or two of its features.

The Alaska Permanent Fund

The Alaska Permanent Fund, created in 1976, is like a mutual fund or unit trust designed to benefit all Alaskans today and tomorrow. Revenue from state oil leases is invested in stocks, bonds, and other assets that generate income and (mostly) grow in value over time. Since 1980, the Fund has paid equal dividends to every Alaskan (including children) ranging from about $1,000 to $3,200 a year. As its creator, former Republican governor Jay Hammond, explained, "I wanted to transform oil wells pumping oil for a finite period into money wells pumping money for infinity."[5] At the end of 2020, the Fund had assets of $65 billion and was pumping money as furiously as ever.

Land trusts

Founded in 1895, the National Trust for England, Wales, and Northern Ireland works to preserve historic and natural places "for ever and for everyone;" it currently owns and manages about a thousand square miles. In 2015 the Trust launched a £10

44

billion plan to "nurse the British countryside back to health" by saving wildlife, planting millions of trees and putting a substantial part of Britain's coastline under conservation easements.[6]

Where I live, in Marin County, California, just north of San Francisco, a large swathe of rural land has survived the seemingly unstoppable spread of highways, suburbs, and malls. Central to this achievement is the Marin Agricultural Land Trust (MALT), which since 1980 has acquired conservation easements covering roughly half the farmland in the county.[7] Much of the funding to acquire the easements comes from a 0.25 percent sales tax approved by county voters. Private owners continue to own and operate their farms, and may sell or bequeath them to whomever they want. However, thanks to the conservation easements, neither they nor subsequent owners may use the land for non-agricultural purposes. MALT makes sure the easement's terms are followed in perpetuity, no matter what the land's future owners, developers, or local politicians may wish to do.

Throughout America, the use of conservation easements has mushroomed in recent years. Tax laws now give incentives for them. The Nature Conservancy uses them to protect forests, wetlands, and prairies. The Department of Agriculture helps farmers and tribes use them to protect farmland. In 2018, a conservation easement database reported over 190,000 easements covering 32 million acres, an area larger than Pennsylvania.[8] That said, the potential uses of conservation easements far exceed these, as we will see.

Worker ownership funds

The idea that workers should own shares in companies they work for has been around a long time. Many private companies issue or sell discounted shares to employees as an incentive to long-term service. In the US today, almost seven thousand companies offer employee stock ownership plans (ESOPs) covering about 28 million workers.[9]

Of course, employee stock ownership is neither universal nor a guarantee of lifelong income. The idea that it should be mandated in *all* companies (or at least large ones) could, however, push it closer to those goals. The most famous, albeit short-lived, manifestation of this idea occurred in Sweden during the 1980s. The "wage-earner funds," as they were called, were the brainchild of economists Rudolf Meidner and Gösta Rehn. Their aim was to gradually transfer ownership of Sweden's major companies from private shareholders to funds managed by labor unions.[10]

Under the original plan, Swedish companies would be required to issue new shares of stock to a wage-earner fund equivalent to twenty percent of their profits each year. At that rate, Meidner calculated, the funds would have majority ownership of most large Swedish companies in about thirty-five years. A milder version of the plan was adopted in 1982, under Prime Minister Olaf Palme, and ran until it was liquidated ten years later by a center-right coalition.

Under the latest iteration of the idea, proposed in 2019 by the UK Labour Party, all British-owned companies with over 250 employees would be required to establish "inclusive ownership funds" for their workers. Every year the companies would issue new stock to the funds equivalent to one percent of their outstanding shares, up to a total of ten percent. Workers would then receive dividends and a right to vote on shareholder-related matters.[11]

An intriguing feature of these plans is their so-called "share levies," which gradually dilute the ownership of existing shareholders but don't affect the companies' cash flow or profitability. The chief shortcoming of the plans is that they benefit only long-term employees of large corporations. They exclude public sector workers, self-employed people, employees of small businesses, stay-at-home caretakers, students, and many others.

Sovereign wealth funds

Sovereign wealth funds, of which there are about eighty worldwide, are state-owned investment funds used to benefit a country's government and economy. Typically, their capital comes from central bank reserves, currency operations, privatizations of state enterprises and/or sale of natural resources. While most sovereign wealth funds are opaque tools of the state, a small number transparently benefit citizens. Norway's contributes four percent of its earnings to the government's annual budget, which helps pay for free education, health care, and other universal services. The Texas Permanent School Fund, founded in 1854, supports public schools throughout the state.

Social wealth funds

A *social wealth fund* is a sovereign wealth fund that, like Alaska's, pays universal dividends. They could as well be called universal property funds. In a 1964 book, Nobel prize-winning economist James Meade proposed a British social wealth fund from which everyone would receive equal dividends, mostly from state-owned enterprises.[12] The idea was too radical for its time and nothing came of it.

Twenty-five years later, Paddy Ashdown, leader of the UK Liberal Democratic Party, proposed a social wealth fund that would hold ten percent of the stock of all large private companies and pay every British citizen equal dividends therefrom. Ashdown contrasted his "citizen's capitalism" with Margaret Thatcher's privatization of everything. Interestingly, his plan went beyond Labour's later "inclusive" ownership funds because it included everyone and offered shares in a diversified portfolio rather than a single firm.[13]

Other versions of social wealth funds keep popping up. In 2016, Stewart Lansley, a British writer, proposed one capitalized by new taxes on capital and share levies as in the Swedish plan.[14] Similar proposals have been floated in the US. In 2009, conservative economist Dwight Murphey proposed a family of independently managed index funds, capitalized by the Federal Reserve, that would pay dividends to all Americans equally.[15] I proposed a somewhat similar fund in 2014.[16] In 2018, progressive think-tank founder Matt Breunig proposed a universal mutual fund that would acquire shares through a mix of share levies, taxes on capital, and money creation by the Fed.[17]

Cap and dividend

Legislation has been introduced in the US Congress to establish a "cap and dividend" system (a.k.a. a "sky trust") to reduce carbon dioxide emissions, a primary cause of global warming. The legislation is based on the premise that the atmosphere belongs equally to everyone. It establishes a schedule of declining limits on selling carbon-based fuels into the economy, culminating in an eighty percent reduction by 2040. Permits to sell the fuels would be auctioned to fuel companies, with the proceeds divided equally among all legal US residents.

An important feature of the model is where the caps are located: not on smokestacks and tail pipes, of which there are myriads, but upstream, where carbon first enters the economy. The idea is simple: if carbon doesn't come *into* an economy, it can't go out. Upstream caps are easy to administer because only a relatively small number of first sellers (about two thousand for fossil fuels entering the US market) need to purchase permits. At the end of the year they pay a penalty if they don't acquire enough of them. That's it. No smokestacks or tailpipes need to be monitored. As with taxes, compliance is a matter for accountants alone.[18]

Personhood for nature

If fictional entities such as corporations can be treated as persons under the law, entitled to almost all the rights of real human beings, why can't animals, trees, and ecosystems be treated that way as well?

In 2017, the New Zealand legislature passed a landmark law

recognizing the Whanganui River, including all of its tributaries, as an "indivisible and living whole" with "all the rights, powers, duties, and liabilities of a legal person," including the right to sue those who harm it. The legislation, which reflects the worldview of many indigenous peoples, was a settlement of long-standing claims by natives whose ancestors lived near the river for centuries. It provides for the appointment of two guardians to "act and speak" for the river, one named by natives and the other by the New Zealand government. However, it doesn't restore ownership of the river to natives, nor is it clear how it will affect their ability to manage the river.[19]

I should note that there is a budding movement worldwide, led by indigenous and animal rights groups, to expand the use of personhood for non-human beings and ecosystems. I support the goals of this movement but worry about its efficacy. I find the personhood model weaker than the trust model, in which specific property rights and fiduciary duties are assigned to trusts in perpetuity. While I have no doubt that guardians will "speak for" their non-human persons, speaking for them is not the same as protecting them. (Remember Dr. Seuss' eponymous children's book in which the Lorax "spoke for" the trees but couldn't stop them from being decimated.) Without property rights and the ability to limit use, the only way guardians can protect a species or ecosystem is to sue abusers after the fact.

The public trust doctrine

Might there be a way to protect nature using principles of universal property, but without using fiduciary trusts or monetizing the use of nature? One possibility is the *public trust doctrine*, a venerable canon that descends from Roman and English law. The doctrine holds that the sovereign of a polity – be it an emperor, monarch, or democratically elected government – has an unshirkable duty to protect nature's gifts for living and future generations.

The doctrine made its way to the United States in the eighteenth century and was included in several state constitutions. For example, Pennsylvania's declares that "Pennsylvania's public natural resources are the common property of all the people, including generations yet to come. As trustee of these resources, the Commonwealth shall conserve and maintain them for the benefit of all the people." Former Pennsylvanian Thomas Paine couldn't have said it better. Alaska's constitution, adopted in 1956, contains a similar clause, which inspired Jay Hammond, the state's Republican governor in the 1970s, to create the Alaska Permanent Fund.[20]

Nowadays, the public trust doctrine is taken to mean that, if a sovereign *fails* to fulfill its duty as trustee of natural resources, it can be sued and ordered to do so by a court. Over the years, suits have been filed in a number of jurisdictions, including a notable one involving Mono Lake, just east of Yosemite National Park in California.

In the 1940s, the Los Angeles Department of Power and Water purchased water rights to four streams feeding Mono Lake and diverted their flows into an aqueduct bound for the city. By 1979, the surface of the lake had dropped forty feet, diminishing wildlife and tourism. A coalition of environmental groups sued the state water board, which had approved the diversion, alleging that it had violated its public trust duty. In 1983, the California Supreme Court ruled for the plaintiffs, Los Angeles was ordered to reduce its diversion, and by 2020 the lake had risen by about eight feet.[21]

While hailed as an environmental victory, the Mono Lake case serves to highlight the limitations of the public trust doctrine as a practical tool. One is that the doctrine can only be applied retroactively, *after* a public agency has failed its duty and damage to an ecosystem has been done. Another is that victory over the state requires a massive legal effort that can cost millions of dollars and last, with appeals, a decade or more. A third is that the chances of success are always iffy.

The underlying problem with the public trust doctrine lies not in the doctrine itself but in the near-impossibility of enforcing it. A trust obligation is not self-enforcing. It requires a trustee with control over the corpus and no conflicts of interest. Government doesn't always pass those tests; it has other things to do and many constituencies to please. That is where independent fiduciary trusts, armed with property rights, could be extremely useful – not to sue the state, but to administer the public trust on its behalf.

The rest of this book focuses on specific applications of universal property that, at scale, could drive markets toward widespread well-being and alignment with nature.

Recall Kate Raworth's vision of containing economic activity between a social floor and an ecological ceiling. It isn't immediately obvious how an unbounded market can do that. Few existing property rights hold markets within that safe and equitable zone, while plenty of property rights tug them beyond it. My broad proposition is that, in order to achieve our meta-economic goals, we need to fortify the doughnut's edges with two applications of universal property: *toll gates* to guard the ecological ceiling and *universal money pumps* to lift the social floor.

Toll gates are checkpoints that adjust chemical flows across the market/nature boundary so that biospheric thresholds can be respected. The relevant property rights here are conservation easements managed by fiduciary trusts. Universal money pumps

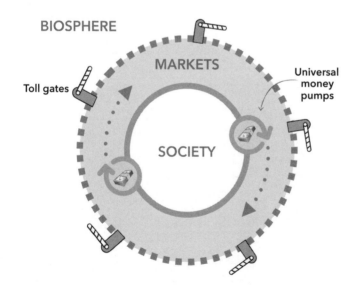

Figure 6 Markets with Toll Gates and Money Pumps

are mechanisms that circulate money to everyone equally, like a drip irrigation system that waters all plants in a garden. They are driven by our right to share income from co-inheritances equally. We will soon see how toll gates and money pumps, backed by universal property, can work independently and together to achieve our economy's meta goals.

5

Interlude for Imagination

Economics is a serious subject. In this chapter, however, we are going to have some fun. We will build imaginary models in which individual and universal property interact, and see what outcomes such models produce. The chapter's goal is to spark an intuitive appreciation of universal property and the impacts it could have in the real world.

Let me assure you that this method of exposition isn't as madcap as it may seem. Thought experiments have been used by philosophers and scientists for millennia. In science, a common approach is to begin with a hypothesis and test it empirically. But where does the hypothesis come from? From previously known facts plus a leap of the scientist's imagination.

Thought experiments aren't new to economics. In 1776, Adam Smith imagined an "invisible hand" that transforms individual self-seeking into collective good. Later, Keynes imagined governments paying people to dig holes and fill them up. And in 1968 Milton Friedman envisioned "helicopter money" falling randomly out of the sky. So I hope you enjoy these brief imaginings and emerge with an intuitive sense of how universal property could make markets do what they must do, but now don't.

Polyopoly

Playing *Monopoly* as a child is what introduced me to capitalism. As an adult, I learned that *Monopoly* was a knock-off of an earlier board game called *The Landlord's Game*, whose inventor, Elizabeth Magie, wanted to promote the ideas of Henry George, an American journalist and thinker whose masterpiece, *Progress and Poverty*, sold over two million copies in the 1880s.

George became famous for his idea that a tax on land should replace all other taxes. The original version of Magie's board game, patented in 1903, came with two sets of rules: in one, a single landlord reaps all the wealth, and in the other, the value of land is equally shared. Players were encouraged to play the game both ways. Needless to say, the games had markedly different outcomes, and players were prompted to ponder why.[1]

As I learned more about complex systems, I realized that *Monopoly* itself is also, if unwittingly, a game with much to teach. It creates an imaginary economy that resembles our real economy in fundamental ways, with markets, property rights, money, competition, and abnormal rewards to monopolists. It differs from our real economy, however, in two striking ways: it starts with perfect equality and goes on to make cash distributions to every player when they pass Go. In other words, every player gets the same amount of start-up capital followed by equal dividends for life.

The essential rules of *Monopoly* are:

- All players start on Go with $1,500 in paper money and receive $200 more each time they pass Go.
- Players can purchase properties they land on and charge rent to other players who subsequently land on them.
- Rents rise rapidly as players acquire adjacent properties and build houses and hotels on them.
- The game ends when one player has all the money and every other player has gone bankrupt. At that point, a kind of "Jubilee" or "re-start" function kicks in, and if the players want to continue playing, they start over as equals.

It is not surprising that a game in which rents rapidly rise leads to extreme wealth concentration; the rules and algorithms are designed to do just that. In this case, they do it by making the wealth-concentrating power of monopoly far greater than the wealth-leveling power of equal endowments and Go payments. For example, the rent for landing on Boardwalk (Mayfair in the British version) starts at fifty dollars and rises to two thousand – a forty-fold increase – when the adjacent property is owned and a hotel has been built. The wide disparity between wealth concentrating and wealth-evening formulae is a feature, not a bug. Even though there are no initial differences in wealth, differences that arise through chance are quickly magnified.

As we know from the so-called "butterfly effect" in complex systems, small changes in rules or starting conditions can have large effects on system behavior. So let's alter a few algorithms in *Monopoly* and see what happens.

CHANGE STARTING CONDITIONS

If *Monopoly* didn't start equally – if, for example, one player started with $15,000 while all others started with $1,500 – it's easy to imagine the consequences. As before, the game ends with one player winning all, but now the game is shorter and less competitive. The illusion of fairness is removed, and no one except the privileged starter really wants to play.

REDUCE GO PAYMENTS TO ZERO

Here, initial fairness is maintained, but players who don't rapidly accumulate property are quickly forced out. Once one player takes the lead, it's hard for laggards to catch up.

REDUCE RENTS AND INCREASE GO PAYMENTS

Now let's try a different tack. If, say, we cut rents by a factor of four (so that the maximum rent for Boardwalk is $500), and multiply Go payments by the same factor, one player still winds up with most of the wealth, but the others don't go bankrupt. This suggests that, by varying rents and Go payments, we could wind up with longer games and less inequality. With such changes in place, we could plausibly change the name of the game to *Polyopoly*.

In *Polyopoly*, there would still be *some* inequality, thanks to chance and subsequent concentration, but it wouldn't be as crushing as in *Monopoly*. And because markets would continue to flourish, there would still be plenty of hotels (which, after all, require customers).

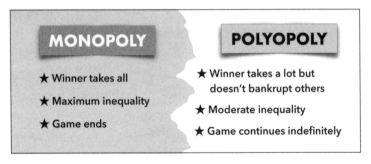

Figure 7

This thought experiment teaches us several things. First, *Monopoly* in its classic form suggests it is possible to have a productive market economy that starts with equal endowments and periodically distributes debt-free cash to all players. It *does no harm* to do those things, up to a point we'll discuss later. On the contrary, such distributions lubricate, stimulate, and extend the game.

Second, the *Polyopoly* version of the game, like Elizabeth Magie's alternate rules, shows what a big difference a few algorithm changes can make. A universal money pump that counteracts Eccles' upward money pump might even enable us to set an economy-wide income equality goal and get close to achieving it.

Gaiaopoly

In our second thought experiment we are going to leap from the human economy to the biosphere. In the 1950s, English scientist James Lovelock invented a device that detects small quantities of chemicals in our atmosphere. This led to the discovery that man-made refrigerants called chlorofluorocarbons were destroying ozone in the stratosphere, thereby allowing cancer-causing ultraviolet rays to reach the Earth's surface. A decade later, Lovelock was hired by NASA to analyze the atmosphere of Mars. Noting that Mars' thin envelope of gas is 95 percent carbon dioxide, he concluded that we didn't need to travel there to know that Mars lacks life.

Lovelock's work for NASA got him thinking about the relationship between life and air on Earth. Since oxygen loves to mate with other elements to form oxides, an atmosphere that is 21 percent oxygen (as ours is) is possible only if oxygen is continuously replenished. That suggests some sort of alliance between the atmosphere and oxygen-exhaling plants, an alliance that must be remarkably fine-tuned since it keeps the supply of oxygen just right. A higher proportion of oxygen in the atmosphere would cause forests to burn all the time, while a lower proportion would snuff out all the animals we love, including ourselves.

Lovelock also pondered the question of how the Earth maintains a friendly-to-life temperature range despite steadily rising heat from the sun. Eventually he developed a hypothesis, since promoted to a theory, which holds that habitable conditions on Earth are maintained by an unwritten partnership between living creatures and non-living chemicals that circulate through the biosphere. At the suggestion of his neighbor, novelist William Golding, he named the theory after the Greek goddess of the Earth, Gaia.[2]

A classic example of the partnership between life and non-living matter is the thermostatic system that keeps temperatures at the Earth's surface within a habitable range. To keep this thermostat working properly requires the density of carbon dioxide in the atmosphere to be just right. If it's too thin, heat escapes and the planet cools; if it's too thick, heat is trapped and the planet warms. The job of maintaining the proper density falls to a planet-wide orchestra of plants and animals. Plants inhale carbon dioxide and exhale oxygen; animals do the reverse. Amazingly, the orchestra has no conductor. Each instrument plays its own tune and the resulting symphony is exactly what our biosphere needs.

Lovelock's notion of Earth as a self-regulating living organism was a bridge too far for many scientists. Darwinists like Richard Dawkins argued that, since the Earth isn't competing with other planets, with the "fittest" surviving, there's no way planetary homeostasis could evolve into existence. Lovelock's response was that homeostasis *can* emerge within a complex system without either natural selection or a divine creator. To buttress his argument he built a computer simulation of an Earth-like system that mindlessly self-regulates for temperature. He called the simulation Daisyworld.

In Daisyworld there are two species, black and white daisies, which thrive at slightly different temperatures. Because of their different coloration, each species reflects and absorbs heat differently, properties that remain constant. The only variable is the input of heat from outside. That input rises 25 percent over time, just as the sun's has.

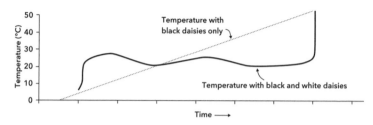

Source: James Lovelock, *Gaia: The Practical Science of Planetary Medicine*
[author's own labels]

Figure 8   Temperature Self-Regulation in Daisyworld

Lovelock let the simulation run to see what would happen. At first, because they thrived at lower temperatures, black heat-absorbing daisies predominated, but as the external heat input increased, white heat-reflecting daises spread. The aggregate biotic shift from heat absorption to heat reflection was enough to offset the rising external heat for quite some time. The result was sustained temperature self-regulation.[3]

Of course, Lovelock's original Daisyworld model, with only two species, is a lot simpler than the real world. So in later work, Lovelock and others built more complex models. What they found was that, as the models became more complex, temperature self-regulation *improved*.

I bring up Daisyworld for two reasons. One is that it shows both how a self-regulating system can work *and* how it can fail. In Daisyworld homeostasis works for a long time but eventually breaks down when the sun's heat gets too hot. A similar fate awaits the real Earth, but long before that happens, a breakdown could be triggered by terrestrial forces such as market failure.

The other reason I bring up Daisyworld is that it is a fore-runner of what today are called *agent-based* computer models. Unlike the macro-economic models that most economists use, which are based on relationships between aggregate data categories, agent-based models start at the lowest level of a complex system and work their ways forward, one agent interaction at a time. Every agent is like an automaton with algorithms prescribing how it will interact with other agents and its environment. Modelers can change the agents' algorithms but can only discover ultimate system behavior by running hundreds of iterations. In the right hands, such models could help assess how universal property agents and algorithms could alter market outcomes.

Imagine a simulated economy with two sets of agents, one whose algorithm is "maximize short-term profit" and another whose operating instruction is "preserve assets for future generations." If profit-maximizers dominate, nature will surely be disrupted. If asset-preservers exert a countervailing force, nature could be okay. But how strong would that countervailing force have to be? Agent-based models could give us clues.

Which leads to two critical questions: if profit-maximizing corporations are the black daisies of market economies, what are the white daisies? And how might we plant a sufficient number of them to make a difference? My answers are: (1) the white daisies are toll gates on nature's edges, managed by fiduciary trusts; and (2) we'll need to plant many of them, like planetary gardeners, until it's clear we have enough.

Googleopoly

Our last thought experiment is a quickie. Consider Google's greatest invention – not its page-ranking algorithm, awesome as that is, but its business model.

What Google sells is clicks – simple actions people take after glimpsing an ad for a few seconds. Using our co-inherited internet, Google captures the fleeting attentions of people who are most likely to click on an ad. Clicks happen and monetized electrons flow from advertisers' bank accounts into Google's. On its YouTube site, which streams videos made by independent creators, Google pays creators about 55 percent of ad revenue and keeps the rest. All this happens automatically, 24/7/365. That is the brilliance of the business model.

Google's business model raises some questions, though. For example, who creates the value of a video – its actual makers or the platform it plays on? Certainly, the platform adds some value, but who created *that* value – the government agency that invented and launched the internet, the schools that taught the scientists and engineers who designed it, its many millions of users, or Google's shareholders? It is not at all clear that the greatest value-creators are Google's shareholders. Their "taking" of value they did little or nothing to create is symptomatic of the larger taking of co-inherited wealth that pervades our entire economy.

Now put on your virtual reality goggles and imagine a Google-like entity that electronically tracks millions of products as they move through markets. Every object that passes through a co-inherited system electronically pays a tiny fee, and every month the fees are distributed equally to everyone. And since you are in virtual reality, imagine that the entity's avatar is an Earth goddess who spreads her benevolence equally among all creatures.

Fantasy? Of course. But the point of these exercises is to kindle insights into how our economy presently works and how we might upgrade it. One shows how flows of money depend on a few simple algorithms that we can alter or counter-balance. Another suggests how humanity might come into homeostasis with nature. And a third shows how modern information technology makes it possible to monitor, monetize, and modify flows of chemicals and money in markets. These insights will, I hope, help you envision the potential of universal property to transform markets as we know them.

6

Universal Money Pumps

Most white Americans who lived through the post-war epoch, with its ever-growing middle class, assumed that each succeeding generation would be better off than the one before. With hindsight, the post-war "golden age" looks less like a never-ending story than an aberration caused by multiple exogenous factors: our global competitors in ruins, babies and suburbs booming, the GI Bill, strong labor unions and the Treaty of Detroit, among others.

It is worth dwelling briefly on the last of these. The so-called Treaty of Detroit was a contract signed in 1950 between the United Auto Workers and General Motors. In return for labor peace, GM agreed to link wages to labor productivity. Once the pattern was set, it spread to other auto companies and unionized industries. The result was that, from 1950 to 1975, Americans' wages rose almost exactly as fast as productivity. A rising tide truly lifted a great many boats.[1]

I mention this "treaty" because it was a *de facto* social contract between millions of workers and large employers. Long ago, Paine's contemporary Edmund Burke opined that society is a contract "between those who are living, those who are dead, and those who are to be born." Lately, there has been talk

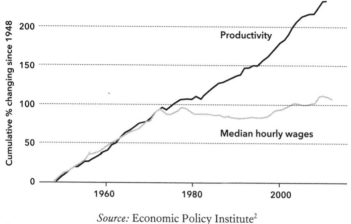

Source: Economic Policy Institute[2]
Figure 9   US Labor Productivity and Wages

in America about our frayed social contract and our need for a new one. This is an encouraging sign. But what needs to be added is the insistence that any new social contracts be, like the Treaty of Detroit, explicit and self-executing.

Actually, as Burke implied, there should be two social contracts, one *inter*-generational and the other *intra*-generational. Social Security is an example of an inter-generational contract that is codified in law and administered by an independent agency. Under it, each working generation supports its predecessors' retirement in return for similar support from its successors. This contract has functioned for over eighty years without missing a payment, an enormous achievement. Still, it addresses only part of our inter-generational responsibility.

The larger part of our duty to our children is to convey

our co-inheritance to them undiminished, if not enhanced. As Burke put it, "temporary possessors and life-renters … should not think it among their rights to … commit waste on the inheritance," a dictum even more pressing in our time than in his. But the question remains: how might we encode this obligation into property rights so that it is binding and self-executing? I will address that in the next chapter.

In any case, the *intra*-generational Treaty of Detroit is long-defunct, and for half a century gains from higher labor productivity – along with takings from co-inherited wealth – have flowed almost entirely to owners of financial capital. I'd be thrilled if the Detroit pact were succeeded by another contract between unions and employers that raised wages broadly, but that seems unlikely. An alternative could be a legislatively enacted "contract with ourselves" that adds a stream of non-labor income to markets.

Universal property and taxes

For more than a century, progressives have sought to redistribute income through the tax code. And graduated income taxes *did* make a difference during the post-war era when the top marginal US rates were 91 percent on income and 77 percent on inheritances. Today's top nominal rates, however, are 37 and 40 percent, respectively, and the average rate paid on inheritances is just seventeen percent.[3]

But besides the political tenuousness of high tax rates, there are two major constraints to redistributing income through the tax system. One is that income taxes take money from people *after* they've acquired it, and such retroactive takings are fiercely resisted. The other is that, while taxes may *take* money from the rich, the redistributive side of the loop is missing. Tax revenues don't flow to anyone directly; they flow into government coffers and thence to wherever politicians choose to send them. Some may be spent on programs that benefit the needy and least powerful, but there are no guarantees.

An alternative to redistribution through taxes is *pre*distribution through universal property, an approach that has several advantages. One is that the money arrives as property income, not as a transfer from other taxpayers. That makes it as stigma-free as other property income.

Another is that much of the distributed money can come from usage fees – for example, from using our atmosphere as a waste dump or our monetary system as a casino. Such fees aren't retroactive takings of received income; rather, they are payments for value received, a.k.a. costs of goods sold. If a corporation or household chooses *not* to burn fossil fuels, it pays no atmospheric dumping fee. If it opts to burn carbon, it pays for atmospheric dumping just as it would pay to use a terrestrial dump.

A third advantage of universal property is that its income sources don't just raise revenue; they can have important corollary benefits, such as reducing harms to nature or excessive speculation and debt.

With these thoughts in mind, let me proffer three potential money pumps built on principles of universal property: (1) a social wealth fund based on co-inherited wealth; (2) a universal inheritance fund linked to personal inheritances; and (3) electronically minted money issued by the central bank directly to all legal residents.

A social wealth fund

A large inheritance can be distributed as a lump sum, variable dividends from assets held, fixed annuities, or any combination thereof. (An annuity is a series of payments that lasts until the end of a recipient's life.) A social wealth fund can be thought of as a lifelong distributor of co-inherited wealth. The size of the distributions would depend on the assets included in the fund and how they "perform" over time.

Paine wanted to create a "national fund," fed by an inheritance tax, that would pay start-up grants to all adults at age 21 and monthly annuities to everyone after age 55. Later, Alaska created a state-wide fund, capitalized by state oil leases and fed by on-going royalties, that pays equal dividends to every state resident from birth to death. Meade, Ashdown and others proposed similar funds that would be financed in a variety of ways. In short, if establishing a national fund that pays equal dividends to everyone is our goal, there are multiple ways to do it.

That said, raising meaningful sums won't be easy. In the eighteenth century, universal start-up grants and old-age annuities could be paid for, per Paine's calculations, by a ten percent tax on individual estates. That's not nearly enough today because everything costs more and we want to pay annuities to everyone, not just the elderly. Still, modern-day funding opportunities abound. As we used to say in California, "There's gold in them hills" – we just have to find it. Here are some places to look.

Make polluters pay

This is the low-hanging fruit for a social wealth fund, and it has the added virtue of protecting nature. The ideal place to start is with the atmosphere.

The best mechanism for charging polluters is to cap the influx of polluting chemicals as far upstream as possible, then sell a declining number of permits. The revenue that could be raised depends on the prices charged, the elasticity of demand and other unknowns. In the case of carbon, revenue estimates range from $700 to $2,400 a year per American.[4] This could be supplemented by revenue from other major air and water pollutants, such as nitrogen, methane, phosphates and non-degradable plastics.

One problem with pollution fees is that they aren't ultimately paid by polluters; they are passed on to consumers in the form of higher prices, which means the poor could be hit hardest. That would be true *without* universal dividends, but *with* dividends, the poor – and indeed a majority – are likely to come out ahead. This has been shown with respect to carbon, with the results in income quintiles depicted below. The progressive impact is due to the fact that the richest quintile accounts for about ten times as much carbon use as the lowest.[5] Its members therefore pay

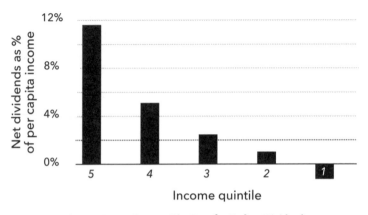

Source: James Boyce, *The Case for Carbon Dividends*

Figure 10   Income Effects of Carbon Cap and Dividend

more in carbon fees than they receive in dividends, while the reverse is true for all other quintiles.

Make oligopolies pay

Until now, anti-monopoly policy in the US and Europe has focused on stopping mergers, prosecuting anti-competitive practices and occasionally breaking up large companies. These aren't bad policies, but they are sporadic, slow, and insufficient. We need more arrows in the anti-monopoly quiver.

One way to think about market concentration is as a negative externality similar to pollution. Companies do their utmost to maximize profit and in the process shift costs and harms to others. The shifted harms of market concentration include higher prices paid by consumers, lower wages paid to workers, and often a loss of innovation. From this perspective, a market concentration fee is analogous to an atmospheric pollution fee.

Another way to think about market concentration is as a diminishment of a valuable co-inheritance – competitive markets – for which compensation is due. Whichever point of view you prefer, the case can be made that market concentrators – monopolies and oligopolies – should contribute to a social wealth fund. A market concentration fee proportional to market share – starting, say, when a company captures twenty percent of a market – is one way to do that.[6] And companies could pay in cash or stock.

Such fees would add to the cost of market concentration, thereby discouraging it, and, if equally shared, would enlarge the dividends that flow to everyone. As with pollution fees linked to dividends, there would be double benefits. We'd get a mix of less market concentration and higher household incomes.

Make speculators pay

As noted earlier, there is far more money swirling around the casino economy than the real one, yet players in the casino get a much freer ride. In the economy of goods and services, taxes are levied not only on income but on sales. In the casino, by contrast, income is taxed at lower rates and sales aren't taxed at all. This makes little sense.

There are several ways this imbalance could be righted. The

simplest and most lucrative would be to insert a tiny fee at the most trafficked points in the monetary circulation system, the clearing houses through which all interbank transfers flow. Right now, the Fed charges less than a dollar to process multi-million dollar transactions between banks – just enough to cover its operating costs.[7] It is a flat fee, not a percentage of the transactions. Imagine, instead, a microscopic fee of one tenth of one percent on each interbank transfer. Applied to a quadrillion dollars, that yields a trillion dollars a year, or about $3,000 per person. The actual revenue would be smaller because the fee will discourage some transactions, but it would still be enormous. When you consider that private banks take between one and three percent of every credit card transaction in the real economy, a minuscule transaction fee in the casino seems entirely reasonable.[8]

A universal inheritance fund

A second universal money pump, smaller than the first, would be aimed at reducing starting-gate inequality, a primary driver of inequality.

According to economists Lawrence Kotlikoff and Lawrence Summers, about eighty percent of US wealth is inherited rather than earned by its owners. French economist Thomas Piketty has put the inherited portion at about sixty percent, while NYU law professor Lily Batchelder places it at around forty percent.[9] Whatever the actual share, it is safe to say that "the top indicator for economic prosperity isn't hard work or intelligence, it's the family you're born into."[10]

America was once, at least rhetorically, opposed to hereditary aristocracy, but we only abolished hereditary *titles*, leaving hereditary *wealth* virtually untouched. It wasn't until the Civil War that we taxed inheritances at all, yet even now the effective tax rate on them is less than one-seventh the average tax rate on labor income. In 2020 Americans are projected to inherit about $765 billion; the expected tax revenue is about $16 billion. That leaves a huge pile of money on the table.[11]

That said, our goal isn't simply to tax intergenerational wealth transfers more heavily but to give every child an inheritance. That requires a distribution on the other side. Paine's plan included an unconditional grant at age 21 of about $18,000 in today's dollars. In 1999, Yale law professors Bruce Ackerman and Anne Allstott proposed a "stakeholder grant" of $80,000 to all high-school graduates, funded by a two percent annual wealth tax.[12]

I can imagine a leak-proof inheritance tax of around fifty percent, with all revenue placed in a universal inheritance fund, the ultimate step in a centuries-long transition from primogeniture to polygeniture. When billionaires and multi-millionaires depart, up to half their estates could pass to their own heirs, with the rest divided among all babies born that year. If the fund captured $300 billion a year and shared it among four million newborns (the recent US average), each would begin life with a $75,000 trust fund, to which rules of prudent management would apply. Millionaires' children would still start on third base, but everyone else's would at least be at the plate. That seems a reasonable way to give all children a fair, if not equal, start as players in a market economy.

I like the link between end-of-life recycling and start-of-life grants because it so nicely connects the passing of one generation with the coming of another. It also connects those who have received much from society with those who have received little; there's justice as well as symmetry in that.

Helicopter money for all

Our monetary system is a *sine qua non* of markets, a public utility to the *n*th degree. It is also a co-inheritance. The primordial questions surrounding this co-inheritance are: to whom should its managers (i.e. the central bank) be accountable, and who gets the windfall (i.e. the seigniorage) from initial issuance of money?

I would argue that a central bank should be accountable to the people broadly, as if they were its beneficial co-owners. Following similar logic, the windfall from initial issuance of money should flow equally to those co-owners, rather than to private banks. If that were done, it would create a third and potentially large universal money pump.

A little-remembered piece of history is relevant here. During the Civil War, New York banks offered to lend money to the Union at rates President Lincoln thought usurious. Instead of borrowing from them, Lincoln had the US Treasury – with Congress' approval – print about $450 million worth of notes (equivalent to about $10 billion today) known as *greenbacks*. There were four ultimate effects of this: (1) the war was paid for and won; (2) business boomed both during and after the war; (3) inflation ran at about fifteen percent a year, high but

Source: Wikimedia Commons

Figure 11 Lincoln's Greenback

not dangerously so, and possibly no higher than would have occurred had the government borrowed the money instead; and (4) there was less debt to repay at the end of the war than there otherwise would have been.[13]

Lincoln was pleased with his monetary experiment and planned to extend it after the war. By that time he had developed a full-blown theory of money that included these elements:

- The original issue of money should be an exclusive monopoly of the national government;
- The national government should not borrow at interest to finance its spending;
- The national government should create and circulate all the currency needed for its own spending and that of households.[14]

Tragically, Lincoln was shot before he could implement these (and other) forward-thinking policies. Private banks retained their money-minting power, along with the right to lend self-created money, at interest, to the government itself. (Why should private banks collect interest for lending government its own money? I have no idea.)

Lately, however, there has been a surge of interest in what is known as Modern Monetary Theory, or MMT. The essence of MMT is that governments that control their own currencies can spend money, up to a point, without raising taxes or borrowing; their only true spending constraint is inflation, which central banks can control for. As Stephanie Kelton, a leading MMT theorist, puts it, "every economy faces a sort of speed limit, regulated by the availability of its productive resources. If a government tries to spend too much into an economy that's already running at full speed, inflation will accelerate. MMT distinguishes this real limit from wrongheaded, self-imposed constraints" such as debt ceilings and pay-for requirements.[15] Lincoln would no doubt have agreed.

In his 1968 paper *The Optimum Quantity of Money* – the one in which he floated the idea of "helicopter money"— monetary theorist Milton Friedman didn't really answer the question, How much money can a government print without triggering inflation?[16] The insight of MMT is that it's not a fixed number or percentage; it's an ever-changing quantity that can only be discovered by printing money and responding to the inflation, if any, that arises. Interestingly, in May and June of 2020, as a response to the Covid pandemic, the Fed and Treasury injected over $3 trillion into the US economy, a good chunk of it directly to individuals, and inflation barely budged.[17]

Robert Hockett, a Cornell law professor who previously worked at the Fed and the International Monetary Fund, is not a full-fledged MMT advocate but accepts its basic analysis. In a 2020 book titled *Money From Nothing*, Hockett explains how the Fed could electronically transfer from $1,000 to $2,000 a month to every American's bank account with minimal systemic risk.[18] He compares such direct transfers to the present system of hoping banks will lend to credit-worthy businesses who will then spend on goods and labor.

"A central bank can operate more effectively and equitably by cutting out the middleman," Hockett argues. Banks often make "more profit betting on speculative derivatives than in lending to you or us," whereas money wired directly to individuals will be spent into the real economy quickly. Further, "this form of 'helicopter money' is debt-free, and far more effective on that account." If inflation does rear its head, the Fed can "freeze" its cash distributions by requiring recipients to save them, with interest, as if they were time deposits.

Imagine, then, a third universal money pump run by a central bank. The bank would inject fresh cash into every individual's account once a month, much as the bank in *Monopoly* does when players pass Go. As in *Monopoly*, these cash injections would benefit not only their initial recipients, but also the businesses and households that get the money when it is spent (economists call this the *multiplier effect*). Governments would also recoup some of the cash through sales and income taxes. As long as inflation is within bounds, it is hard to see who loses.

Universal property and taxes, again

You may have noticed that some of the proposed revenue sources for universal money pumps resemble taxes. This might seem to contradict my earlier argument that universal property *pre*distributes income through property rights rather than *redis*tributes it through taxes. I grant that there is room for confusion here. To get clarity, we must distinguish between government as a *collector* of money and co-inherited wealth as its actual *source*.

Paine chose government to collect ground rent in his 1796 proposal. The actual asset he wished to charge for was land, a gift of nature to all, but collecting such rent annually from many thousands of landowners nationally would have been a difficult task in those days. From a practical perspective, it made more sense for a national government to collect the rent once, at a landowners' death, and to do so as part of the probate process, with local courts as allies.

Paine also included personal property, such as structures sitting on land, for two reasons: the difficulty of separating the value of structures from that of land, and the fact that much of the value of *all* property is attributable to society rather than individual effort. Thus, despite his use of government to collect money, the actual sources of money were naturally and socially created wealth.

Similar considerations may well apply today. In a world perfectly suited to universal property, every traded product would be digitally encoded and its sellers appropriately charged for their use of co-inherited wealth. Electronic money would then whiz into the bank accounts of everyone equally. This would be a grander version of the arrangements of artists' organizations, like the American Society of Composers, Authors, and Publishers (ASCAP), which monitor public performances and collect fees for use of works by their members. But simpler expedients might also make sense.

For example, Herbert Simon floated the idea of a flat income tax of seventy percent, of which half would support federal programs at present levels and half would pay per capita dividends of about $8,000 a year.[19] Similarly, 2020 presidential candidate Andrew Yang proposed a ten percent value-added tax (which the US currently lacks) to pay $1,000-a-month Freedom Dividends to all.[20] In both cases, a single national tax would feed a universal money pump.

The idea of using a value-added tax, or VAT, to fund universal dividends raises some interesting questions. What a VAT taxes is the value added by each business at its stage of the production process. Though consumers don't see it the way they see added-at-purchase sales taxes, they are the ones who ultimately pay it. It is, in other words, a hidden tax on consumption.

Every country in the European Union collects a VAT of at least fifteen percent; the average is 21.3 percent. The primary objection to a VAT is that is regressive. Though rich people consume more *per capita* than poor people, and therefore pay more VAT in absolute terms, as a percentage of income, a VAT hits the poor hardest, even if food is exempted. However, as with a regressive carbon fee that is returned to everyone equally, the net effect of a VAT linked to equal dividends is progressive – the poor gain most as a percentage of income.[21] This makes it a plausible candidate for a universal money pump.

Another interesting question raised by a VAT is, why should we tax value *added*? Adding value is what we *want* businesses to do. Wouldn't we be wiser to tax value *subtracted,* as suggested by Pigou, or as Paine would have framed it, to charge for private use of co-inherited wealth? One reason we don't follow Pigou's or Paine's prescription is computational. A business can readily calculate its value added by deducting its costs of production from its sales; there is presently no way it can calculate its value subtracted or use of co-inherited wealth. But there's little doubt we could develop reasonable equivalents.

Using government to collect fees from co-inherited wealth would open up a host of new money streams. For example, corporate surtaxes that could be paid with shares are a potentially effective way to capitalize a social wealth fund. The share levies could be linked to specific events such as initial public offerings, acquisitions and stock buy-backs, or simply be a small percentage of market capitalization each year. An advantage of share levies is that they don't affect corporate cash flow or profitability; they simply dilute the equity of existing shareowners and reallocate it to those from whose co-inherited wealth is taken – a readjustment that is long overdue.

More money for the national fund could also flow from a FICA-like (Federal Insurance Contributions Act) levy on non-labor income. Right now, the US Social Security system collects a payroll tax of 12.4 percent, half deducted from workers' paychecks and half initially paid by employers but ultimately paid by workers in the form of lower wages and consumers in the form of higher prices. According to the Tax Policy Center, two-thirds of US workers pay more in payroll taxes than in regular income taxes.[22] Yet even though the IRS deems wages to be "earned" and property income to be "unearned," there is no equivalent tax on unearned income. That workers contribute to our old-age security system, while wealth owners don't, seems like a gaping hole waiting to be filled.[23]

There are other places to look for monetizable co-inherited wealth. Intellectual property rights – patents, copyrights, and trademarks – have exploded in recent decades, and their monopolistic rents constitute a huge gift to the technology, pharmaceutical, and entertainment industries. I have no problem protecting – without charge – authors, inventors and other individual creators, but companies that massively benefit from intellectual property protection should pay for some of the value that protection adds. Figuring out how to do that is an interesting challenge.

Similarly, the internet is a socially created asset without which companies like Amazon, Google, Facebook, and Netflix couldn't exist. How much should such companies pay us to use this asset? How much should advertisers and data extractors pay? These are complex questions with potentially fruitful answers.

The ideal social wealth fund – like any decent private equity fund – would have a mixed portfolio of assets, including rights to usage fees from co-inherited wealth, corporate shares that reflect such usage, and more. It would be designed to grow over time and pay dividends from current income. There is room for much creativity in designing such a fund. Perhaps if we shrink the financial casino, some ex-Wall Street whizzes might take up this task – with bonuses if universal dividends grow.

Brief case

Let me now make a brief economic case for universal money pumps. Two cases, really – macro- and meta-economic. By the former I mean an old-fashioned case that universal money pumps will boost GDP. By the latter I mean a more meaningful case that they'll boost individual and social well-being, within the bounds of nature.

The macro case is straight-forward. By reducing our now-chronic scarcity of household income, universal money pumps will keep the wheels of our economy turning at as close to full employment as we can get these days.

There is nothing novel about this argument; it is basic Keynesianism. Indeed, two Keynesian think tanks, the Roosevelt and Levy Institutes in the US, modeled the potential macro-economic impact of universal income and found that GDP would be higher than it otherwise would. That's because the universal pumps would shift money *from* those who would put most of it into the casino *to* those who would spend it on real goods and services. That shift not only boosts GDP but spreads it around more evenly.[24]

The meta-economic case is two-fold. First, by reducing financial precarity for a majority of the population, universal money pumps will increase the well-being of millions. Social cohesion will also improve. Second, as we'll see in the next chapter, dividends from ecosystem rents can help align markets with nature.

Objections

Over the years, I've heard more than a few objections to universal income in any form. Here are the main ones and my responses.

We can't afford it

This argument calculates the cost of paying everyone a certain amount of money each year, comes up with a very large number and concludes that it is prohibitive. The problem with this argument is its assumption that more spending on one priority necessarily means less spending on another, as if money were a pile of coins that can only be used once. In reality, money is a flow, and what matters as much as its quantity are its direction and velocity.

What universal money pumps do is *change the direction* of our real economy's money flow, and boost its velocity as well. The velocity goes up because lower- and middle-income households get more money and spend it. And the direction changes because universally pumped money enters the economy from the bottom rather than the top, even if the quantity of money is the same.

What about money available for government? Universal money pumps, as envisioned here, don't diminish current government revenue or require the cutting of any existing government programs. Once established, they circulate money that didn't previously circulate. And eventually, they *increase* government revenue by stimulating the economy and creating a new stream of dividends to tax.

What if some universal property equivalents are new taxes that could otherwise fund new government programs? Do we have to choose, say, between a Green New Deal and monthly dividends for everyone?

I would answer this question by positing that major new government programs should be funded by raising the rates of existing taxes, cutting spending elsewhere or borrowing, and that money from co-inherited wealth should flow first to its rightful owners and *then* be taxed and used by government. That way, we could have *both* universal dividends and a Green New Deal, without fighting over tax revenue. Universal dividends would then be an integral part of a Green New Deal, making sure its benefits are universally and transparently shared.

*Universal income promotes individual consumption over
public investment*

At first glance, universal income leads to more private spending on private goods, and progressives sometimes dismiss it for that reason. "Better to have government spend money on infrastructure than to let individuals spend it on flat-screen TVs," is a trope I've heard more than once. Environmentalists also worry that giving people money to spend on TVs and hamburgers is bad for the planet.

On the last point, denying individuals the ability to spend money is not going to save the planet; the much more efficient place to constrain consumption is upstream, at the edges between nature and markets. It is there that limits can be set and prices raised to depress the use of Earth-harming goods throughout an economy.

A related point involves the distinction between public and private goods. A private good is anything an individual spends money on; a public good is a service provided by government that serves a large number of people. Examples include roads, sewers, education, and national defense. Broadly speaking, progressives like public goods while conservatives prefer the private kind (except for defense and law enforcement).

Where does universal income fit within the public goods framework? My answer is two-fold. First, as previously noted, the two types of spending aren't mutually exclusive: it is possible to do both. More importantly, universal income *is* a public good, precisely because it is universal. Yes, some of it may be spent on TVs, though a lot more will be spent on basic necessities. But regardless of what individuals do with the money, what makes universal income a public good is that it enhances economic security and social cohesion.

As British economist Guy Standing has put it, "Economic security is a natural public good – your having it does not deprive me of it, and we all gain if others have it too." In addition, universal dividends strengthen social cohesion by demonstrating that "we are all part of a national community sharing the benefits of the collective wealth we created over our collective history."[25] To which I'd add that, if there is anything we need more of right now, it is social cohesion.

Universal income will be inflationary

There are two prongs to this argument. One is that anything that substantially increases the flow of money to households will cause prices to rise. The other is that "printing" money will lead to the kind of hyper-inflation that undermined German democracy in the 1920s.

With regard to the first prong, more money in the pockets of households *will* raise prices if supply can't keep up with demand (recall the earlier discussion of Modern Monetary Theory). But now that we are in the surplus stage of capitalism, that is unlikely to happen. When an economy's capacity to produce exceeds its capacity to buy, boosting demand will create its own supply. If households have extra money to spend, extra goods and services will be produced for them to spend it on. And prices won't be greatly affected until production can't catch up with demand.

With regard to Weimar-phobia, it is important to remember the reason Germany printed so many *deutschmarks* after World War I: the Allies imposed unpayable reparations on it. Universal money pumps won't impose a comparable cash-draining burden. Moreover, central banks will be able to fine-tune the amount of money they issue to households, just as they fine-tune their infusions into banks.

Universal income will undermine the work ethic

In popular lingo, universal income will make people lazy. This objection has been empirically tested a number of times, and there is no evidence that it is true, at least when payments are modest. To the contrary, evidence from the US, Canada, and Finland indicates that it isn't.

Thus, a study in Alaska found that payment of universal dividends for forty years had no measurable effect on the state's employment rate.[26] Similarly, data from a 1970s guaranteed income experiment in Manitoba, Canada, found "no significant effect on employment for primary earners," but some reduced employment among married women who used their extra income to finance maternity leaves, and young adults who used it to stay in school longer, both of which I'd deem positive outcomes.[27] And in a recent Finnish experiment, about half the participants received a basic income and half didn't. After two years, the group that received a basic income worked slightly more hours than the group that didn't.[28]

Other evidence comes from the US coronavirus relief package that disbursed generous unemployment payments –

sometimes exceeding previous wages – to millions of Americans in the spring of 2020. A preliminary analysis by economists Hilary Hoynes and Jesse Rothstein found that states with high unemployment benefits saw less of a drop in employment than did those with lower benefits.[29]

Further, the "discouragement of labor" argument doesn't account for the value of work people do *outside* the mone-tized labor market, a contribution to well-being that universal income could well increase. And finally, even if the quantity of paid work *is* somewhat reduced in the future, that might not be a bad thing: more time outside the labor market would increase human well-being, as long as total income (labor plus non-labor) is maintained. In fact, if we want a shorter paid work week, a reliable source of non-labor income is almost a pre-requisite.

Giving money to people who don't need it is wasteful
This is the "fiscal responsibility" argument against universal income. But only two percent of Americans earn more than $400,000 a year, the line below which President Biden pledged never to raise taxes.[30] Denying them "universal" dividends might be penny wise but would almost certainly be pound foolish.

What could be "saved" is no more than a tiny percentage of the money distributed – even less if dividends are taxed and people are allowed to opt out or required to opt in. A few percent is a small price to pay for the moral clarity and political durability created by universality. More fundamentally, only by embracing *everyone* as equal co-inheritors can we assert our right to share what is legitimately ours. Without that assertion, we are back to welfare and charity as the only ways to supplement labor incomes. And in most countries, they will never be enough.

Universal property diminishes the role of government
Universal property is a response to some failings of government, but it doesn't require any diminishment of government. It is true that, as a vision for the future, an expansion of universal property could serve as an alternative to an expansion of government. But if government expanded the fabric of property rights to reduce inequality and harm to nature, it wouldn't *need* to get much bigger than it now is. In other words, government and universal property are complementary. We need both.

7

Toll Gates at Nature's Edges

For centuries we've bent nature to markets; now it's time to bend markets to nature. The question is how.

The Earth is heading for a crash because we humans are unable to moderate our use of its vital ecosystems. It is clear by now that we – and especially our profit-maximizing corporations – will never do this voluntarily. Self-imposed constraints are required to make us do what we *must* do together but don't *want* to do on our own. Ideally, those constraints should be as fair, transparent, user-friendly, and self-enforcing as possible.

One approach to constraining collective behavior is rationing. That is what many countries did during World War II, when all available resources were needed for war efforts. Civilians received allotments for petrol, basic foods, and cigarettes, and paid for them with cash and coupons. Black markets arose, but the basic objective of rationing was met. Consumption was limited and in most cases people felt the systems were reasonably fair.

Rationing is typically a temporary imposition that people accept in an emergency and remove when the emergency ends. What we need today is a self-constraining system adaptive and durable enough to get us through the Anthropocene. This long-term challenge will require more than a Green New Deal or global Marshall Plan, which include no constraining mechanisms. With nature now the scarcest resource, we *need* to limit the market's use of it, without cramping the market's style. Universal property, I contend, is the best way to do that.

Universal property is a multi-function tool. With one set of fittings, it can combat economic inequality. With another, it can protect nature in perpetuity. In this chapter we'll focus on the second set.

Protecting nature in perpetuity is a daunting task. No human society in the modern age has been able to do it. Not even the world's richest countries, despite passing many environmental laws, have come close. Indeed, the more we stare at the fundamental problem – the insatiable demands of capitalism confronting the inviolable thresholds of nature – the more insoluble it appears. Still, universal property, properly deployed, can take us a long way.

Let's think for a moment about boundaries. About half a century ago, biologist Garrett Hardin wrote an influential essay called *The Tragedy of the Commons* in which he argued that humans will always overuse commons because it's in their self-interest to do so and commons have no way to stop them. The only possible ways out of this tragedy, he argued, are private or government ownership of commons.[1]

What Hardin overlooked, however, is that there is more than one kind of commons and more than one way to manage them. The kind of commons he described is called an *open access* commons. It is perfectly possible to have a *fenced* commons in which access is limited, and just as possible to have a management structure that sets and enforces those limits.[2] Putting a managed fence around a commons does not make it any less a commons: it still belongs to everyone and can be used by anyone, just not all at once, or all the time, or without paying.

Hardin's so-called tragedy of the commons is actually a mischaracterization of two other tragedies: a tragedy of the market, which has no way of curbing its own excesses, and a tragedy of government, which fails to protect nature because exploiting corporations are powerful and future generations don't vote. The appeal of universal property is that it can avert both tragedies simultaneously.

One consequence of the Anthropocene is that we humans must become players in Earth's homeostatic orchestra. To do that, we'll need market mechanisms, analogous to James Watt's steam engine governor, that "read" nature's thresholds and respond by reducing human harm.

Recall the Raworth doughnut's outer border. On one side lie nature's immutable physical laws; on the other, humanity's mutable property laws. The border itself, however, is essentially a Wild West where no one is in charge. There is continuous movement of matter and energy across it, but very little accounting or regulation of that movement. The market's takings from the biosphere are mostly unpriced and unchecked, as are its dumpings of harms into it.

Suppose, however, that the market/biosphere boundary

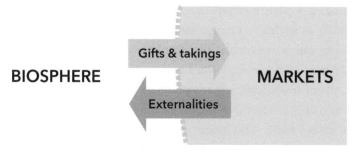

Figure 12 The Market-Biosphere Boundary Today

had fences with gates on them. These gates could be fully shut or adjustably open, depending on the biosphere's tolerances. When they are open, they'd be subject to metered use. Prices of nature-disturbing goods and activities would then rise, spurring businesses and households to use less of them. We'd get the economy-wide benefits of rationing without individual quotas, coupons, or queues. And the integrity of the biosphere would be protected for generations to come.

The notion of an ungoverned boundary between nature and markets raises a slew of interesting questions. The most important involve the governance of this frontier. Who should control the gates, and with what powers, instructions, and accountability?

Few would contend that profit-maximizing corporations should control nature's gates; that would be like putting foxes in charge of hen houses. In the prevailing worldview, the leading – indeed only – candidate for this job is government. And yet, based on its track record, government isn't ideal for this responsibility either. Its loyalty to nature will rarely be as strong as its fealty to large corporations, wealthy donors and living voters. Inevitably, the biosphere will suffer.

There is, however, a third option: put nature's gates in the hands of trusts legally accountable to future generations. This is arguably as close as we can get to putting them in the hands of nature itself. The instructions to the trusts would be that long-term ecosystem preservation, not short-term financial gain, comes first. If we build a network of such fiduciary trusts, with sufficient property rights to make markets listen, we just might constrain ourselves from destabilizing the planet we co-inherited.

The job of these trusts would be relatively straightforward. They wouldn't have to manage entire ecosystems, a herculean task. Rather, their sole function would be to monitor critical ecosystems and appropriately adjust the gates between them and markets. What they'd actually manage, in other words, would not be nature itself but human activity that encroaches on it.

Imagine a network of such gates, each managed by a government-chartered trust. Trustees could be appointed in a number of ways. Some could be chosen by voting members, others by sitting trustees, and others by public officials. Regardless of how they are appointed, trustees would serve extended terms and be removable only for cause. Most importantly, they'd be bound by law to be one hundred percent loyal to future generations. If they act with any less loyalty than that, they'd be subject to penalties enforceable by courts, including removal.

The market power of the trusts would lie in the property rights they hold, which are essentially super-sized conservation easements. Some of the easements could be acquired through donations or purchases, but most should be granted at no cost by government. Such twenty-first-century easement grants could be compared to the nineteenth century land grants to railroads and twentieth century airwave grants to broadcasters, with this notable difference: the grants of conservation easements to fiduciary trusts would not be a privatization of co-inherited wealth, as the earlier grants were. Rather, they would be a sharing and preservation of co-inherited wealth with future generations foremost in mind. That is the main reason the trusts shouldn't pay for their easements.

A second reason is that there are no pre-existing owners to compensate. In this respect ecosystem trusts differ from many land trusts, which *do* have to compensate existing owners for easements. No one, however, owns a right to pollute or otherwise diminish co-inherited ecosystems.

How would the trusts manage cross-boundary traffic? It would depend on the ecosystem and the activities that most harm them. One model is the upstream caps embodied in cap and dividend legislation. Another is the congestion pricing system in central London, where license plate-spotting cameras automatically charge each car owner's bank account. A third is the scannable coding system that links products to cash registers everywhere. All suggest that humans are clever enough to meter almost anything we do or use, and charge for such activity accordingly.

Another important question is where to place the toll gates. The biosphere has many thresholds, and some are more important or imperiled than others. In 2009 a team of scientists led by Johan Rockström of the Stockholm Resilience Centre identified ten planetary thresholds beyond which humans ought not to tread. These include our atmosphere's capacity to absorb greenhouse and ozone-destroying gases, our soil's abilities to absorb nitrogen and phosphorous, species diversity, habitat loss (including forests), and freshwater use. We now know enough, the scientists declared in 2015, to propose quantified limits for eight of these boundaries, three of which we've already crossed and two more of which we are dangerously close to.[3]

Based on such research, it is possible to imagine toll gates on all major greenhouse gases, deforestation, agricultural chemicals, and land use conversions. Peer-reviewed scientists would advise on thresholds, and fiduciary trustees would decide how many permits to issue. Toll gates would then be adjusted, and the process would repeat as needed. There would rarely be incontrovertibly "right" amounts of usage or prices. Most of the time there'd be a range of probabilities and approximations, and the trustees' duty would be to err on the side of safety.

Another set of boundary questions involves money. If biosphere-disrupting permits are sold, large new streams of money will be generated. Ideally, they would flow into social wealth funds and investments in ecosystem preservation or restoration. How much should flow to each?

In my view, a significant amount of revenue recycling is a *sine qua non* for any boundary management system that must

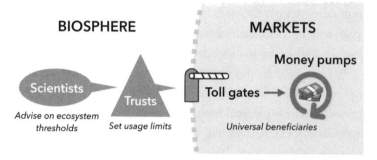

Figure 13 How to Align Markets with Nature

endure over time. If everyone pays in proportion to their ecosystem use, and everyone gets an equal amount of money back, a majority will come out ahead (since ecosystem use skews toward the well-off minority). If, on the other hand, prices rise and people *aren't* transparently and equitably reimbursed, usage constraints will either be too weak to matter or collapse altogether.

Objections

There are three main objections to limiting humanity's use of nature, with toll gates or any other mechanism. Here they are with my responses.

Ecological limits will make us poorer

This objection, promoted by extractive and polluting industries, is meant to persuade (or scare) everyone who hopes for a higher standard of living. I have two responses, which are not mutually exclusive. One is that economic growth will continue even with border constraints. The second is that we can increase human well-being without growth in physical throughput.

With regard to the first response, let me say that I am an optimist about economic growth; I believe it can be maintained within ecological boundaries. Humans are a clever and ambitious species. If we tell ourselves, "Here is our economic playing field, its boundaries and goal posts – now let's play ball!," we will do so with grit and enthusiasm. Washington DC imposed height limits on buildings and flourished nonetheless. Los Angeles cut its water use after losing the Mono Lake case and now consumes less water than it did in 1980 despite adding three million people.[4]

How will markets adapt to reduced use of nature? I can't tell you exactly, but I can tell you that, regardless of our relationship to nature, the goods and services of the twenty-first century will differ markedly from those of the last. Fifty years ago, the five most valuable US corporations were Exxon, General Motors, IBM, AT&T, and Eastman Kodak; today they are Apple, Amazon, Google, Facebook, and Microsoft, none of which existed in 1970. Joseph Schumpeter called this *creative destruction*. It is what markets naturally do, and what makes me optimistic about future adaptation. Regardless of limits on our use of nature, some industries will shrivel and others will rise in their place. The factor most affecting GDP while this happens will be the steadiness of consumer demand. That's why it is crucial to link trusteeship of nature's gates to dividends derived therefrom.

The second part of my response is that, even if GDP *is* reduced by gates on nature, human well-being – our economy's ultimate goal – can still flourish. Imagine an economy in which people travel less in petrol-guzzling cars, health care is organized rationally, work weeks are shorter, stress is lower, and non-labor income flows regularly to everyone. In such an economy, well-being will surely rise. My point is that, when economies reach the surplus stage, GDP growth isn't necessary for greater well-being. Economic security, less inequality, and more free time matter more.

A trusteeship system can be compromised too

I've made the argument that government can't be relied on to protect nature over the interests of businesses and living voters, but where is the evidence that fiduciary trustees can do better? To put this another way, what if the real problem isn't the failure of markets or government but the self-centered nature of humans – a biological trait that is unlikely to change?

I don't assume the beneficence of human nature. I assume that humans are both self-seeking and cooperative, and that the way we behave *en masse* is driven by the tugs of society, government, and markets. I agree with James Madison in the *Federalist Papers* that "if men were angels, no government would be necessary," and that "in framing a government which is to be administered by men over men … you must first enable the government to control the governed, and in the next place oblige it to control itself."[5] The same logic, I'd argue, applies to markets. Like governments, they need built-in checks and balances.

Most democratic governments include independent branches that can check each other. In my view, a trusteeship "branch" of markets would be the functional equivalent of the judicial branch of government. Like judges, trustees would be appointed for long terms and be removable only for cause. And just as judges must adhere to law and facts rather than the desires of voters or lobbyists, so trustees would be bound to the needs of nature and future generations. While it is true that, on occasion, judges have been bribed, this doesn't happen frequently, and I assume the same would hold for trustees. After all, if we can't trust judges and fiduciaries, whom *can* we trust?

What about all the other things we must do to save the planet?
Aren't they more important than this?
The list of things we need do to save the planet is endless, and everybody has their favorites. We can debate the relative virtues of each, but whatever else we do to protect the planet, we must also limit our harmful uses of nature, and do so sooner rather than later.

Constructive measures, as envisioned in a Green New Deal, are essential, but we can't overlook harm-constraining measures. Indeed, without them, we'll never fix the market failure that got us into the Anthropocene in the first place. Moreover, constraints aren't just a negative force; they are also a positive force, driving markets to innovate. As has aptly been said, necessity is the mother of invention.

Donald Trump over four years weakened almost every major environmental regulation that had been adopted during the preceding forty years.[6] Perhaps some will be restored, but his presidency highlighted the fundamental weakness of government regulation: it follows the political winds and is *always* under attack by well-funded corporations and lobbyists.

What would protect ecosystem trusts is a combination of fiduciary duty and universal dividends. Fiduciary duty would drive trustees' adjustments of the toll gates, while universal dividends would sustain political support for the constraining system as a whole. If there is a surer way to align human economic activity with nature, I haven't seen it. As James Boyce has written with respect to carbon dividends, "Because everyone pays according to their use of the atmosphere, and receives dividends based on their equal co-inheritance, the arrangement would be widely perceived as fair. It is hard to imagine any other carbon-limiting policy that could sustain broad public support in the face of significant escalation in fossil fuel prices."[7]

8

The Politics of Universal Property

I once gave a briefing to Congressional staff on how a declining upstream carbon cap with auctions and dividends would tilt our economy from dirty to clean fuels while strengthening our middle class with non-labor income. At the end of my technical presentation I opined that voters would love the dividends and show their gratitude to every politician who supported them. When it was time for questions, one liberal House aide ventured, "I don't understand. Where are the programs? There's no money for programs here."

I left the briefing in a state of befuddlement. I had assumed that liberal environmentalists would quickly grasp the ecological, economic, and political virtues of cap and dividend. What I hadn't foreseen was the staying power of old mental models. When liberals spot a problem that needs fixing, they instinctively revert to government regulation and spending. The idea that we might transform markets without a plethora of regulatory or spending programs was as alien to the liberal House aide as the idea of higher taxes is to conservatives.

Later I stumbled across a concept known as the "Overton Window," the brainchild of a young libertarian named Joseph Overton who died in 2003. According to Overton, there is only a narrow range of policies that politicians can support at any given time. Though the actual spectrum of policy options may be quite wide, only a sliver lies within the zone of political acceptability. That sliver shifts over time, as norms and ideas do, but politicians don't move it, they only act within it.[1]

I find this idea useful in considering the politics of universal property because it helps distinguish between the present and the near future. Thus, my proposition is not that universal property is within the Overton Window today. Rather, it is that it *could* be there in a few years, given forces at play today.

Until this point I've treated universal property as an economic idea – a framework for upgrading markets so they achieve their meta goals. Now it is time to explore its place in political thought and practice.

As a political idea, universal property appeals both conceptually and with real deliverables. Conceptually, it takes the old American motto, *E pluribus unum* ("out of many, one"), to mean not only that we are better off united as *states;* we are also stronger and freer when we unite as members of society and co-inheritors of many valuable assets.

With regard to deliverables, universal property offers two big ones: early-in-life inheritances and reliable cash flow until death. These deliverables would flow to everyone and palpably improve our individual and national well-being. No one would be excluded because of race, gender, employment status, or income, and the gains – while equally shared – would disproportionately help the poor.

Beyond these monetary deliverables, we'd gain comfort from knowing that we are harming nature less, and pride in belonging to a society that cares for all its members. And perhaps most importantly, we'd boost social unity rather than division. So many politicians and policies pit one set of people against others. Universal property would directly and frequently remind everyone that, when it comes to our economy and planet, we are all in the same boat together.

Prospects

To assess the political prospects of universal property, we need to look backward as well as forward in time. What we find is that the idea has roots as well as wings.

The roots of universal property are ancient. "The meek will possess the earth," says Psalm 37. God "hath given the world to men in common" echoed John Locke.[2] Then came Thomas Paine, who combined nature's gifts with social creations and invented a brilliant method for monetizing and sharing both.

Throughout the nineteenth century, as European settlers of America headed west, they fought for and won the right to claim homesteads by living and working on them. After the frontier closed, the federal government insured millions of thirty-year mortgages so that Americans could buy homes in cities and suburbs. This wasn't universal property, but it gave everybody a shot at *some* property.

There are roots of universal property in the UK as well, starting with the Magna Carta, which established fisheries and forests as *res communes*, and continuing to then Labour Chancellor Gordon Brown's creation of "baby bonds" in 2005, giving every British new-born a tax-exempt bond worth up to £500. (Bond issuance was halted by then Conservative Chancellor George Osborne five years later.)[3] In between and since, there have been proposals by James Meade and Paddy Ashdown for social wealth funds, as well as a slew of recent proposals for a universal basic income.[4]

It is worth delving into Meade's 1964 book, *Efficiency, Equality and the Ownership of Property*, for the light it sheds on universal property today. Meade was writing at a time when strong trade unions bolstered labor's share of national income, but he saw that automation and global competition would soon undermine this. Without a source of property income, he argued, workers' economic gains wouldn't last. While supportive of labor unions, the welfare state and public ownership of key industries, Meade called for – in addition to all of the above – a "property-owning democracy" in which every citizen would own income-producing property. Time has shown that Meade, like Paine, was prescient.[5]

As important as the roots of universal property are the wings it is sprouting at this moment. In 2020, a virtually unknown American entrepreneur named Andrew Yang launched a grassroots campaign for President on a platform of universal $1,000-a-month "Freedom Dividends," funded by a value-added tax. Ignored at first by pundits, his campaign out-fundraised several major candidates and lasted until the sixth nationally televised Democratic debate. Media coverage of the idea of universal income soared. Then, when the coronavirus hit, even Republicans supported sending cash to everyone, no questions asked. The Overton Window on universal cash distribution had noticeably shifted.

At the same time, the Fed and the Bank of England have been inching in a similar direction. Until recently, their preferred monetary tool was to raise or lower interest rates. Following the 2008 financial meltdown, after interest rates got as low as they could go, the central banks unveiled a new tool called "quantitative easing," or QE, a deliciously inscrutable way to pour trillions of dollars into private banks in the hope that they'd productively lend them.

Not surprisingly, the trickle-down part of QE didn't work very well. But QE was a novel idea that soon led to more novel ideas, one of which is "QE for the people" – distributing new money directly to individuals. Robert Hockett has proposed this in the US, and a group called Positive Money is campaigning for it in the UK.[6]

On the ecological front, political winds are also shifting. One reason bills to curb carbon dioxide emissions repeatedly died in Congress is that Republicans almost universally opposed them. In 2018, a group of Republican grandees, led by former Treasury Secretaries James Baker and George Schultz, proposed a rising tax on carbon emissions coupled with a return of every dollar to the American people.

The Baker-Schultz plan was endorsed by more than three thousand economists, including N. Gregory Mankiw, former chair of President George W. Bush's Council of Economic Advisers. "One of my favorite words is *panacea,* " Mankiw said at a press conference launching the plan. "Usually it is used in the negative – something is *not* a panacea. This is the closest thing I know to a panacea. It solves lots of problems at once. Maybe it's not a complete panacea but it's as close to one as I've ever seen."[7]

Interestingly, in 2006, Mankiw had founded the Pigou Club, a self-described "elite group of economists and pundits with the good sense" to support Pigovian taxes. What Mankiw had since come to see was that the solution to climate change lay not in Pigou alone, but in Pigou *plus Paine*. Pigou's prescription creates the higher prices that discourage external harms; Paine's provides the extra income that makes the higher prices palatable. When the two are bundled, well-being rises on both sides of the ledger. But without Paine, there's no gain.

The future prospects of universal property are linked to the future intensities of economic inequality, social division, and humanity's cumulative impact on nature: the more intense these get, the greater the need – and, one hopes, demand – for universal property will be. Here I focus on that demand.

The chief hindrance to the demand for universal property is outdated mindsets. With regard to economic inequality, today's proposed remedies mostly involve labor income: adding jobs and raising wages. These remain worthy goals, but they aren't enough. A second front needs to be opened for non-labor income. Most of today's jobs pay too little to sustain a large middle class, and tomorrow's bode little better. So if we want a middle class today and in the future, we *must* spread non-labor income around. And there are only two ways to do that.

One is to tax Jill to pay Jack, or in economic language, to redistribute income using taxes and means-tested transfer payments. This approach is unpopular on both ends. Jill resents the taking of her hard-earned income; Jack resents the indignities of being on welfare.

The other way is to pay both Jill *and* Jack dividends from their co-inherited wealth. The first approach divides society, the second unites it. Jay Hammond, a Republican, took the second approach in Alaska, and it was a huge success. Why not do the same with co-inherited assets besides oil?

The old story about non-labor income – that only the well-behaved needy (and, of course, the rich) should get it – doesn't get us very far. As *The Economist* noted recently, "America is bogged down in the interminable exercise of separating the deserving poor from the undeserving."[8]

A more unifying story is that our right to co-inherited wealth precedes and undergirds our right to non-labor income: we are entitled to equal shares of co-inherited wealth not because we are needy, but because we are born equal. These co-inherited shares, in turn, can be converted into grants, dividends, and/or annuities. This story not only paves the way to more non-labor income, equally shared; it also assures its durability.

I can envision future debates between proponents of tax-based, means-tested transfer payments and universal dividends from co-inherited wealth. Each side will have good points to

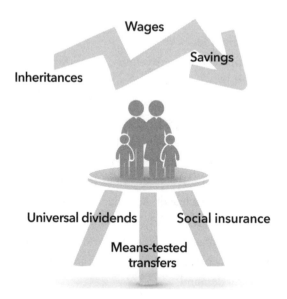

Figure 14 Income Security Stool

make. However, this should not be a winner-take-all contest; both are needed. Universal dividends should not *replace* means-tested payments, as some have argued; rather, both should be legs of an income security stool that, in one way or another, lifts all people throughout their lives.

What about humanity's cumulative impact on nature? Here again we need a new political front. Recent environmental campaigns have focused on tightening or defending regulations, stopping this or that destructive project, and calling for a Green New Deal. All are important. But no one yet talks about giving ourselves the property rights we need to protect entire ecosystems in perpetuity, as the Anthropocene requires. That is seen as a bridge too far.

However, protecting ecosystems with property rights is a more attainable goal than it may seem. Local conservation easements are a tried and proven tool. Applying such easements to ecosystems is a leap in scale but not design. Why *couldn't* a fiduciary trust like the National Trust or Nature Conservancy hold ecosystem conservation easements on behalf of future generations? And why *not* grant them free of charge the way we granted land to railroads not that long ago? The cost to taxpayers would be zero, and down the road there would be dividends. But the main benefit is that we'd have science-driven gates on human disturbances of nature, something nature itself will increasingly demand.

What about scale?

A question that overhangs the politics of universal property is, how much of it do we need? Could a little go a long way – as in *Polyopoly*, a few algorithm changes do? Or do we need a lot of it to make a difference?

In the best scenario, a modest amount of universal property, installed in just the right places, could steer markets toward greater equality and alignment with nature. It's also possible, even probable, that a large dose is needed. The truth is that we can't know how much is needed until we install some and see what happens. Which means the way forward is to start small and keep adding as long as we need to and can.

That said, it is possible to be somewhat more specific. Let's focus first on universal dividends, then on contraints upon our use of nature.

Sometime before the 2016 presidential election, Hillary Clinton read my book *With Liberty and Dividends for All*, which proposed a national social wealth fund inspired by Alaska's. As she later wrote, "I was fascinated by this idea, as was my husband, and we spent weeks working with our policy team to see if it could be viable enough to include in my campaign ... Unfortunately, we couldn't make the numbers work. We decided it was exciting but not realistic, and left it on the shelf."[9]

Had I been contacted by Clinton's policy team, I would have noted that *no one* can accurately project social wealth fund revenues because their proposed sources are new, variable, and unpredictable. More importantly, this inability to predict *doesn't matter*. The numbers will always "work" because dividends will never exceed revenue: the fund will distribute only what it earns. Further, no existing programs need be cut to pay for it. And if, after a few years, the public clamors for higher dividends, assets can be added to the fund. The important thing politically is to get the fund started.

Proponents of a fixed basic income often toss out numbers like $500 or $1,000 a month. With universal dividends, there is no need to pre-set a number. Dividends will vary from year to year, and that's okay. It guarantees that future generations won't be burdened with today's dividend costs. And, as Clem Tillion, one of the architects of the Alaska Permanent Fund, once put it, "Variability makes people aware it's *their* money, not the government's."[10]

If I were to plot a political strategy for building a social wealth fund in the US, I'd start by reviewing our history of contributory social insurance. The idea (imported from Bismarck's Germany) was first discussed by academics prior to World War I. Pilot programs were launched in Ohio and Wisconsin in the 1920s. And in 1935 Congress passed the landmark Social Security Act. The initial payroll tax was two percent, split between workers and employers; benefits were around $30 a month; and large categories of workers were excluded. Starting in 1936 and periodically ever since, social insurance (including Medicare, added in 1964) was enlarged step-by-step and now accounts for about ten percent of GDP. And it has all but eliminated extreme poverty among the elderly.

I'd then suggest that social *inheritance* has become a necessary and proper sequel to social *insurance,* and that it can be installed in a similar sequential manner. This has two implications:

- There must be a committed core group keeping its "eyes on the prize" – enough universal property to make a fundamental difference.
- For the first decade, architecture matters more than size. Get the property rights, institutional designs, and algorithms right. Eventually, political support will grow and so will universal dividends.

How high could universal dividends go? The upper limit would come when the rate of inflation approaches a level deemed safe by the Fed. My premonition, though, is that universal dividends would level off at a point above which means-tested benefits make more sense, perhaps $8,000 per person per year in 2020 dollars, the level Herbert Simon hypothesized. I'd note here that Norway's sovereign wealth fund, the world's largest, has financial assets of about $1 trillion. If it paid dividends at the rate of four percent, each of Norway's roughly five million residents would receive about $8,000 a year. That seems a reasonable level of universal dividends in mature economies that also have tax-funded safety nets.[11] To meet needs above that level, means-tested programs make more sense.

Switching to the toll gate side of the question, estimating the required scale is harder. The scaling variable here isn't money but *rates of reduction* of these harms to nature. The minimal goal is to reduce these harms rapidly enough to avert the most catastrophic effects of climate change. Universal property can't achieve this goal without other public policies, but the degree to which it can help is significant and scalable.

One of the big obstacles here is that no nation by itself can align humanity with the biosphere. This is an all-nations job, yet global climate negotiations, which began thirty years ago in Rio de Janeiro, have thus far been discouragingly slow.

What universal property can contribute to averting climate catastrophe are three things: first and most obviously, steadily declining limits on human use of fossil fuels; second, dividends which retain popular support for that declining use; and third, border adjustment fees which could allow a few large countries plus the EU to do what global negotiations seemingly can't.

Let me expand on the last piece. Border adjustment fees' primary purpose is to protect domestic companies from paying higher pollution prices than foreign competitors. But border fees not only make domestic political and economic sense; they also have the knock-on effect of inducing other countries to raise their internal pollution prices. That way they can keep those fees at home rather than pay them to economic rivals.

The "growth strategy" I'd propose for toll gates on nature is therefore the same as that for dividends: start with low-hanging fruit (which here means carbon toll gates with dividends and border fees) and add more as political opportunities arise. Admittedly, installing toll gates is less sexy than building new infrastructure (though dividends make them sexier), but it has to be done just as aggressively. The faster old behaviors are phased out, the faster new ones will take their place.

Two last points about scale. One is that toll gates on nature will not generate enough revenue on their own to fund universal money pumps at their optimal level. If we want universal dividends to be meaningful, we must include revenue from socially created wealth as well.

The second point is that no one can say at this moment, or perhaps ever, what the right boundaries are between markets and nature; we can only approach them by trial, error, and self-correction. What *can* be said, though, is that, whatever the boundaries are, we need an *institutional structure* to continuously administer them. Without such a structure, we won't stay within our ecological ceiling no matter how well-intentioned we may be.

For many years, political debate in the US and UK has been gridlocked between advocates of less government and more. A market economy interspersed with universal property bypasses that polarized stalemate. It is a *hybrid* of capitalism and socialism, and of nature's and humanity's economies, blending the best of each.

Hybrids have much to commend them. In biology, their physiological vigor is often greater than their progenitors'. Similarly, in human societies, economies that produce the most well-being, like those in Scandinavia, blend markets and private enterprise with wage solidarity and generous welfare states.

In this case, universal property's virtues include not only what it adds to markets, but just as importantly, what it preserves in them. With universal and private property in balance, markets would retain the vitality and dynamism they currently possess. Prices would still send signals, innovation would still flourish, entrepreneurs would still start businesses, and governments would not do much more than they currently do. In short, we'd get the upsides of markets without their tragic flaws.

The greatest virtue of a hybrid economy, however, may be political. It is rare in America and Britain when one "ism" completely dominates all others, and even rarer when one dominates for a long time. Usually, compromises have to be made and political winds shift. A market economy with universal property could emerge as a twenty-first century compromise – or synthesis if you prefer – and then endure because, once begun, its support grows. Such a synthesis would have been unthinkable ten years ago, but it no longer is today.

9

The Adjacent Possible

The case for universal property can be summarized briefly. Universal property is needed to supply what markets currently lack: self-regulating brakes on external harms and money pumps that lift everyone up. Without such additions, inequality will split us apart and nature will become our mortal enemy.

What is special about universal property is that it reaches beyond transient public policies and into the legal fabric of markets themselves. But it is fair to ask, can it be installed in this century?

I was born four months after Pearl Harbor. My first childhood memory is of victory over Japan being celebrated in the streets of Manhattan. So I am familiar with the time span from the end of World War II to today. It is a time span I can put my mind around. Which helps me imagine possible paths to the end of this century. Same time span, opposite direction.

When I began working on this book several years ago, I assumed we would have a major crisis in the not-too-distant future, followed by a period during which rapid changes would occur. My hypothesis was that, within such a period, universal property could take root. As I conclude writing, that period –

thanks to a virus – has begun.

There can be little doubt that the world today is at an inflection point. But what can be said about the next eighty years, other than that they are up for grabs?

One clue comes from a theory posited by paleontologists Niles Eldredge and Stephen Jay Gould in 1972. Based on fossil records revealing long periods of evolutionary stasis, Eldredge and Gould contended that "the history of evolution is not one of stately unfolding, but a story of homeostatic equilibria, disturbed only rarely by rapid and episodic events of speciation."[1] They called this pattern *punctuated equilibrium*, and it seems to apply not just to biological evolution but to political and economic evolution as well.

Punctuated equilibrium takes us beyond the Overton Window, which applies only during periods of equilibrium. As to what happens *after* a punctuation, a hint comes from mathematical biologist Stuart Kauffman.[2] According to Kauffman, if a punctuated system doesn't completely collapse, it shifts into a period of chaos during which new ideas and experiments compete for traction. Eventually, a new equilibrium emerges that adapts many features of the old system but incorporates critical novelties.

The new equilibrium, Kauffman argues, is neither predetermined nor entirely random; rather, it is one of a limited set of *adjacent possibilities*. Such adjacent possibilities are a consequence of path-dependence. Just as a complex system's present configuration is rooted in past ones, so future configurations will be rooted in the present one. The "winning" adjacent configuration, whatever else can be said about it, must therefore be both similar to the failed system yet different enough to overcome its fatal flaws.

At this moment, our menu of adjacent economic possibilities includes authoritarian oligarchy like Russia's, state capitalism like China's, welfare capitalism like Scandinavia's, Charles Koch-style capitalism with minimal regulation and taxation, and a hybrid market economy with universal property. Which adjacent possibility emerges in which countries is, of course, entirely unpredictable, but my hypothesis is that the hybrid candidate is on the short list for countries like the US and UK. It is close enough to our present system to qualify as adjacent, yet distinct enough to be a viable successor.

I can envision a future scenario that looks something like this:

- Universal property begins in the 2020s with a package of carbon fees, financial transaction fees and debt-free central bank money disbursed equally to everyone. Such a package generates from $2,000 to $3,000 per person per year, comparable to the Alaska Permanent Fund.[3]
- In subsequent years, as political tides shift, the social wealth fund is enlarged with more ecosystem usage fees, oligopoly fees, and corporate stock acquired through levies.
- The demand for higher dividends after that then grows as automation replaces labor, climate change undermines economic stability, and universal dividends become popular.

In a hybrid market economy filled with universal property, much that is good in our present economy would continue. In particular, the primacy of private over state property would endure, with this caveat: private property itself would be divided into two classes, individual and universal. The meta-directions markets then take – toward more or less well-being, and more or less disruption of nature – would then depend on the relative strengths of the two kinds of property.

Can a society choose the adjacent possibility it wants? It is my belief that when a complex system includes humans, it is possible for humans to *influence*, if not decide, which adjacent possibility emerges. This happens all the time when businesses launch new products. The question here is, can it happen in a whole economy?

Milton Friedman believed that "when a crisis occurs, the actions that are taken depend on the ideas that are lying around."[4] He and other conservative intellectuals tried repeatedly, and with some success, to use crises to implant their ideas in many countries. That isn't a bad strategy for universal property, but it must be accompanied by vocal popular demand and the shifts in mindset described earlier.

For years, the British filmmaker Richard Attenborough, producer of the biopic *Gandhi,* wanted to make an equally epic movie about Thomas Paine. He hired a top-rank screenwriter, Trevor Griffiths, to write the script, and tried unsuccessfully to raise $65 million to produce it. Afterward, the screenplay was published as a book and became a minor classic among cinephiles.[5]

In the final scene, Paine's grave in New Rochelle, New York, lies open and we hear him reading from *Agrarian Justice*. "There must grow, and soon, a system of civilization ... so organized that not a man or woman born but shall inherit some means of beginning the world and see before them the certainty of escaping the miseries that have always accompanied old age ...." Then:

> The shot tilts suddenly, reveals a modern highway, heavy with traffic, ripping past New Rochelle. Mixes with the southbound flow to today's New York City and its images of wretchedness and affluence ...

Is it possible that Paine's fullest vision – an equal sharing of naturally and socially created wealth – can be realized in this century? There can be no guarantees, but I'd venture that the odds are considerably greater than zero. It has taken more than two hundred years, but for all the reasons I've given in this book, I believe the time for Paine's vision is coming soon.

Notes

1 What is Universal Property?

1 Herbert Simon gave two estimates of the share of present US wealth that is attributable to co-inherited social capital: 80 and 90 percent. In "UBI and the Flat Tax," *Boston Review*, October 1, 2000, http://bostonreview.net/forum/basic-income-all/herbert-simon-ubi-and-flat-tax, he estimated it was 90 percent. In his last public lecture, he dropped it to 80 percent, the figure I have quoted. https://inst.eecs.berkeley.edu/~cs195/fa14/assets/pdfs/simon_last_lecture.pdf.

2 William Easterly and Ross Levine, "Tropics, Germs, and Crops: How Endowments Influence Economic Development," *Journal of Monetary Econo*mics, 50 (1), (January 2003), http://www.nyudri.org/research-index/2003/tropics.

3 Robert Costanza et al., "The Value of the World's Ecosystem Services and Natural Capital" (1997), *Nature*, 387, May 15, 1997, London: 253 ff., https://www.researchgate.net/publication/229086194_The_Value_of_the_World's_Ecosystem_Services_and_Natural_Capital.

4 The most recent "cap and dividend" legislation was introduced in June 2019 by Senator Chris van Hollen (D-Maryland) and Rep.

Don Beyer (D-Virginia), https://www.vanhollen.senate.gov/imo/media/doc/Healthy%20Climate%20and%20Family%20Security %20Act.pdf.

5 As Guy Shrubsole recounts in W*ho Owns England?*, thirty entities – families, corporations, duchies, and individuals – own half the land of England. This goes back to the eleventh century, when William the Conqueror replaced the existing aristocrats with his own. Their heirs, in turn, have ruled the English countryside ever since. As the sixth Duke of Westminster once put it, the best way to succeed in Britain is to "have an ancestor who was a very close friend of William the Conqueror."

6 Thomas Paine, *Agrarian Justice* (1796), is available in many editions, collections and web sites, including the US Social Security Administration's website, https://www.ssa.gov/history/paine4.html.

2 Why Markets Fail

1 N. Gregory Mankiw, *Principles of Economics*, 7th edn. (2015), Cengage Learning, Stamford CT, p. 12.

2 E. F. Schumacher, *Small is Beautiful: Economics as if People Mattered* (1973), Harper & Row, New York, pp. 46 ff.

3 Kate Raworth, *Doughnut Economics* (2017), Chelsea Green Publishing, White River Junction VT, pp. 9 ff.

4 Marinner Eccles, *Beckoning Frontiers: Public and Personal Recollections* (1951), Alfred A. Knopf, New York, p. 76.

5 Matthew 13:12.

6 Zuckerberg's wealth fluctuates along with the price of Facebook

shares. The figure of $90 billion reflects his wealth on September 21, 2020. Daily updates can be found at https://www.forbes.com/profile/mark-zuckerberg /#1d6db 2353e06.

7 Janet Lowe, *Warren Buffett Speaks: Wit and Wisdom from the World's Greatest Investor* (2007), John Wiley and Sons, Hoboken NJ, p. 212.

8 Nicola Davison, "The Anthropocene Epoch: Have We Entered a New Phase of Planetary History?" *Guardian,* May 30, 2019, https://www.theguardian.com/environment/2019/may/30/anthropocene-epoch-have-we-entered-a-new-phase-of-planetary-history. Also Paul Crutzen, "Geology of Mankind" (2002), *Nature,* 415 (23), https://doi.org/10.1038/415023a.

9 Arthur C. Pigou, *The Economics of Welfare* (1920), Macmillan, London, p. 17.

10 A summary of Minsky's thinking can be found in his paper, *The Financial Instability Hypothesis* (1992), Levy Economics Institute, Annandale-on-Hudson NY, available at http://www.levy.org/pubs/wp74.pdf. An assessment of Minsky's impact, including Paul Krugman's quote, can be found in "Minsky's Moment," *The Economist,* July 20, 2016, https://www.economist.com/schoolsbrief/2016/07/30/minskys-moment. See also L. Randall Wray, *Why Minsky Matters* (2016), Princeton University Press, Princeton NJ.

11 See David Colander, *Complexity and the History of Economic Thought* (2008), Middlebury College, Middlebury VT, http://sandcat.middlebury.edu/econ/repec/mdl/ancoec/0804.pdf.

12 Michiyo Nakamoto and David Wighton, "Citigroup Chief Stays

Bullish on Buyouts," *Financial Times*, July 9, 2007, https://www.ft.com/content/80e2987a-2e50-11dc-821c-0000779fd2ac.

3 Twenty-First-Century Realities

1 John Kenneth Galbraith, *The Affluent Society* (1958), Houghton Mifflin, Boston, p. 2.

2 Theodore Geisel ("Dr. Seuss"), *The Lorax* (1971), Random House, New York.

3 Michael McLeay, Amar Radia and Ryland Thomas, "Money Creation in the Modern Economy," *Quarterly Bulletin* 2014 Q1, Bank of England, London, https://www.bankofengland.co.uk/quarterly-bulletin/2014/q1/money-creation-in-the-modern-economy.

4 Rana Foroohar, *Makers and Takers: How Wall Street Destroyed Main Street* (2016), Crown Business, New York, p. 6.

5 Fedwire annual transaction volumes can be found at https://www.frbservices.org/resources/financial-services/wires/volume-value-stats/annual-stats.html. Other US interbank clearing-houses include the Clearing House Interbank Payments System (CHIPS) and the Automated Clearing House (ACH) network.

6 John Maynard Keynes, *The General Theory of Employment, Interest and Money* (1936), Macmillan, London, p. 159. Available online at http://www.hetwebsite.net/het/texts/keynes/gt/chap12.htm.

7 Federal Reserve Bank of St. Louis, *Nonfarm Business Sector: Labor Share*, https://fred.stlouisfed.org/series/PRS85006173.

4 The Jobs of Universal Property

1 *State of the Commons* (2003), Tomales Bay Institute, Point Reyes Station CA, http://www.onthecommons.org/sites/default/files/stateofthecommons.pdf.

2 Schumacher, *Small is Beautiful*, op. cit., p. 51.

3 From Cardozo's opinion in *Meinhard v. Salmon* (1928), a case in which the New York Court of Appeals held that partners in a business owe fiduciary duties to one another, https://casetext.com/case/meinhard-v-salmon.

4 Edward N. Wolff and Maury Gittleman, *Inheritances and the Distribution of Wealth* (2011), US Bureau of Labor Statistics, Washington, Table 6, p. 34, https://www.bls.gov/osmr/research-papers/2011/pdf/ec110030.pdf.

5 Jay Hammond, "Diapering the Devil: A Lesson for Oil Rich Nations" (2005), https://www.cgdev.org/sites/default/files/archive/doc/books/GovernorsSolution/Ch2_GovernorsSolution.pdf, p. 19.

6 Patrick Barkhan, "How the National Trust Saved Our Coastline," *The Telegraph*, March 13, 2015, https://www.telegraph.co.uk/travel/destinations/europe/united-kingdom/articles/How-the-National-Trust-saved-our-coastline/.

7 Marin Agricultural Land Trust, http://malt.org/our-impact/.

8 National Conservation Easement Database, https://www.conservationeasement.us/. Accessed on 9/22/2020.

9 Mary Josephs, "Fast Facts on ESOPs," *Forbes*, June 19, 2018, https://www.forbes.com/sites/maryjosephs/2018/06/19/fast-facts-on-esops/#960599b42b1b.

10 "Wage Earner Funds in Sweden," Aarhus University, https://nordics.info/show/artikel/wage-earner-funds/. See also Rudolf Meidner, *Employee Investment Funds: An Approach to Collective Capital Formation* (1978), Allen & Unwin, London, and "Why Did The Swedish Model Fail?"(1993), *Socialist Register*, https://socialistregister.com/index.php/srv/article/view/5630.

11 Richard Partington, "How Would Labour Plan to Give Workers 10% Stake in Big Firms Work?" *Guardian*, September 24, 2018, https://www.theguardian.com/business/2018/sep/24/how-would-labour-plan-to-give-workers-10-stake-in-big-firms-work. For an American perspective, see Lenore Palladino, "Inclusive Ownership Funds for the United States" (2015), Roosevelt Institute, New York, https://rooseveltinstitute.org/2019/05/15/inclusive-ownership-funds-for-the-united-states/.

12 James Meade, *Efficiency, Equality and the Ownership of Property* (1964), Allen & Unwin, London. On the impact of Meade's ideas see Stuart White, "Citizen Ownership: The Lost Radicalism of the Centre?" *Open Democracy*, November 8, 2013, https://www.opendemocracy.net/en/opendemocracyuk/citizen-ownership-lost-radicalism-of-centre/.

13 Paddy Ashdown, *Citizens' Britain: A Radical Agenda for the 1990s* (1989), Fourth Estate, London.

14 Stewart Lansley, *A Sharing Economy: How Social Wealth Funds Can Reduce Inequality and Balance the Books* (2016), Policy Press, Bristol.

15 Dwight Murphey, *A Shared Market Economy: A Classical Liberal Rethinks the Market System* (2009). Kindle and https://shared-

marketeconomy.com/introduction-to-a-shared-market-econ omy-a-classical-liberal-rethinks-the-market-system/table-of-co ntents/chapter-1/.

16 Peter Barnes, *With Liberty and Dividends for All* (2014), Berrett-Koehler, San Francisco.

17 Matt Bruenig, *A Social Wealth Fund for America* (2018), People's Policy Project, Washington DC, https://www.peoplespoli-cyproject.org/projects/social-wealth-fund/.

18 US Congressional Budget Office, *An Evaluation of Cap-and-Trade Programs for Reducing US Carbon Emissions* (2001), Washington DC, https://www.cbo.gov/publication/13107, p. 6.

19 Jeremy Lurgio, "Saving the Whanganui: Can Personhood Rescue a River?" *Guardian*, November 29, 2019, https://www. theguardian.com/world/2019/nov/30/saving-the-whanganui-can-personhood-rescue-a-river.

20 Pennsylvania Constitution, Section 27, https://law.justia.com/ constitution/pennsylvania/; Hammond, "Diapering the Devil," op. cit., p. 7.

21 Harrison Dunning, *The Mono Lake Decision: Protecting a Common Heritage Resource from Death by Diversion* (1983), Environmental Law Reporter, 13 ELR 10144, Environmental Law Institute, Washington DC, https://elr.info/sites/default/files/articl es/13.10144.htm.

5 Interlude for Imagination

1 On the fascinating history of the board game *Monopoly*, see Mary Pilon, *The Monopolists* (2015), Bloomsbury Publishing, London.

2 James Lovelock, *Gaia: A New Look at Life on Earth* (1979), Oxford University Press, Oxford.

3 A good discussion of Daisyworld can be found at https:// en.wikipedia.org/wiki/Daisyworld. See also James Lovelock, *Gaia: The Practical Science of Planetary Medicine* (1991), Gaia Books Limited, London.

6 Universal Money Pumps

1 For an analysis of the Treaty of Detroit see Frank Levy and Peter Temin, *Inequality and Institutions in 20th Century America* (2007), National Bureau of Economic Research, Cambridge MA, http:// www.nber.org/papers/w13106.

2 Josh Bivens and Lawrence Mishel, *Understanding the Historic Divergence Between Productivity and a Typical Worker's Pay* (2015), Economic Policy Institute, Washington DC, p. 4, https://files. epi.org/2015/understanding-productivity-pay-divergence-final. pdf.

3 Lily Batchelder, *Leveling the Playing Field between Inherited Income and Income from Work* (2020), NYU Law and Economics Research Paper No. 20–11, 2020, p. 43, https://www.hamilton project.org/assets/files/Batchelder_LO_FINAL.pdf.

4 James K. Boyce, *The Case for Carbon Dividends* (2019), Polity, Cambridge UK, p. 60.

5 Ibid., p. 74.

6 In 1968, University of Chicago law professor Richard Posner (later a US appeals court judge) proposed a surtax of 20 percent on monopoly profits in excess of a fair rate of return as deter-

mined by a government agency. At the time, the basic corporate income tax rate was 52 percent. Thus, Posner argued, "the public would have the satisfaction of knowing that 72 percent (normal corporate income tax plus surtax) of any monopoly profits would be extracted from the monopolist and used for public purposes." Richard A. Posner, *Natural Monopoly and Its Regulation* (1968), 21 Stanford Law Review 548, p. 640, available at https://chicagounbound.uchicago.edu/cgi/viewcontent.cgi ?article=2861& context=journal_articles. As of this writing, the basic corporate income tax rate is 21 percent and there is no monopoly surtax.

See also Marc Jarsulic, Ethan Gurwitz and Andrew Schwartz, *Toward a Robust Competition Policy* (2019), Center for American Progress, Washington DC, for a more recent proposal for a monopoly tax, https://www. americanprogress.org/issues/economy/reports/2019/04/03/467613/toward-robust-competition-policy/.

7 Fedwire fees for 2020 can be found at https://www.frbservices.org/resources/fees/wires-2020.html.

8 This approach to transaction pricing was adapted from Scott Smith, *The New Operating System For the American Economy* (2017), self-published on Amazon.com. Though his numbers seem wildly inflated to me, his core concept makes sense. I should note that a monetary transaction fee differs from a tax on trades in stocks, currencies and other securities, another frequently discussed option.

9 Facundo Alvaredo, Bertrand Garbinti and Thomas Piketty, "On the Share of Inheritance in Aggregate Wealth: Europe

and the USA, 1900–2010" (2017), *Economica* 84, Blackwell Publishing, Oxford, pp. 239–60; Laurence J. Kotlikoff and Lawrence Summers, "The role of intergenerational transfers in aggregate capital accumulation" (1980), National Bureau of Economic Research, Cambridge MA, https://www.nber.org/papers/w0445.pdf; and Lily Batchelder, "Tax the Rich and Their Heirs," *New York Times*, June 24, 2020, https://www. nytimes.com.2020/06/24/opinion/sunday/inheritance-tax-inequality.html.

10 Josh Hoxie, quoted in "US Inequality is only Getting Worse," *Business Insider*, February 23, 2019, https://www.businessinsider.com/is-income-inequality-caused-by-inheritance-generational-wealth-2019.

11 Batchelder, *Leveling the Playing Field*, op. cit., p. 46.

12 Bruce Ackerman and Anne Allstott, *The Stakeholder Society* (1999), Yale University Press, New Haven CT.

13 Steven Russell, *The US Currency System: A Historical Perspective* (1991), Federal Reserve Bank of St. Louis, St. Louis MO, traces the evolution of US currency from Lincoln's greenbacks to today's Federal Reserve Notes. https://files.stlouisfed.org/files/htdocs/publications/review/91/09/Currency_Sep_Oct1991.pdf. For US inflation rates from 1800 to the present, see https://www.officialdata.org/org/us/inflation/1800?amount=1#:~:text=The%20U.S.%20dollar%20experienced%20an,of%20%2419.63%20over%20220%20years.

14 Michael Rowbotham, *The Grip of Death: A Study of Modern Money, Debt Slavery and Destructive Economics* (1998), Jon Carpenter Publishing, Charlbury UK, pp. 220–1. Rowbotham

includes a two-page statement of Lincoln's monetary thinking, attributed to Senate Document 23, 1865, that I was unable to find in any repository of Lincoln or Senate documents. It is possible that he took the statement from Gerald McGeer, *The Conquest of Poverty* (1933), Garden City Press, Quebec City, Quebec, Canada, who used it as well, but also wrote that he modified Lincoln's words while "scrupulously maintaining" his ideas.

15 Stephanie Kelton, "Learn To Love Trillion-Dollar Deficits," *New York Times*, June 9, 2020, https://nyti.ms/3cScgME. See also Kelton's book, *The Deficit Myth: Modern Monetary Theory and the Birth of the People's Economy* (2020), PublicAffairs, New York.

16 Milton Friedman, *The Optimum Quantity of Money and Other Essays* (1969), Aldine Publishing, Chicago.

17 Brent Schrotenboer, "US is Printing Money to Help Save the Economy from the COVID-19 Crisis," *USA Today*, May 13, 2020, https://www.usatoday.com/in-depth/money/2020/05/12/coronavirushow-u-s-printing-dollars-save-economy-during-crisis-fed/3038117001/.

18 Robert Hockett and Aaron James, *Money From Nothing* (2000), Melville House, Brooklyn NY, p. 175.

19 Simon, "UBI and the Flat Tax," op. cit.

20 For more information about Andrew Yang's Freedom Dividend plan see http://www.fdmath.com.

21 William Gale and Benjamin Harris, *Creating an American Value-Added Tax* (2013), Brookings Institution, Washington DC, https://www.brookings.edu/research/creating-an-american-value-added-tax/.

22 Robert Williams, *Most Americans Pay More Payroll Tax Than Income Tax* (2016), Tax Policy Center, Washington DC, https://www.taxpolicycenter.org/taxvox/most-americans-pay-more-payroll-tax-income-tax.

23 According to the National Academy for Social Insurance, a 12.4 percent surtax on unearned income could raise about $265 billion a year. William Arnone, Peter Barnes and Renée Landers, *Assured Income* (2019), National Academy of Social Insurance, Washington DC, https://www.nasi.org/sites/default/files/research/Final%20Copy%20Assured%20Income%20.pdf, p. 32.

24 Michalis Nikiforos, Marshall Steinbaum and Gennaro Zezza, *Modeling the Macroeconomic Effects of a Universal Basic Income* (2017), Roosevelt Institute, New York, https://rooseveltinstitute.org/modeling-macroeconomic-effects-ubi/.

25 Guy Standing, "Why the World Should Adopt a Basic Income," *The Economist*, July 4, 2018, https://www.economist.com/open-future/2018/07/04/why-the-world-should-adopt-a-basic-income.

26 Damon Jones and Ioana Marinescu, *The Labor Market Impacts of Universal and Permanent Cash Transfers: Evidence From The Alaska Permanent Fund* (2018), National Bureau of Economic Research, Cambridge MA, https://www.nber.org/papers/w24312.pdf.

27 Evelyn Forget, *The Case for Basic Income in Canada* (2012), https://www. researchgate.net/publication/275648949_The_Case_for_Basic_Income_in_Canada.

28 Heikki Hiilamo, "The Basic Income Experiment in Finland

Yields Surprising Results," *Nordic Welfare News*, University of Helsinki, May 7, 2020, https://www. helsinki.fi/en/news/nordic-welfare-news/the-basic-income-experiment-in-finland-yields-surprising-results.

29 Noah Smith, "Pandemic Aid Helps Make the Case for Basic Income," *Bloomberg Opinion*, July 7, 2020, https://www.bloomberg.com/opinion/articles/2020-07-07/coronavirus-financial-aid-helps-make-case-for-basic-income.

30 CNN, "How Close Are You to the Top 1%?" https://money.cnn.com/calculator/pf/income-rank/index.html.

7 Toll Gates at Nature's Edges

1 Garrett Hardin, "The Tragedy of the Commons," *Science*, December 13, 1968, https://science.sciencemag.org/content/162/3859/1243.

2 For a deeper discussion of what Hardin misunderstood about commons, see Elinor Ostom, *Governing the Commons: The Evolution of Institutions for Collective Action* (1990), Cambridge University Press, Cambridge UK.

3 "Boundaries for a Healthy Planet," *Scientific American*, April 2010, pp. 54–60. Updated in 2015: https://science.sciencemag.org/content/347/6223/1259855.

4 For historical Los Angeles water usage see https://data.lacity.org/A-Livable-and-Sustainable-City/Historical-LADWP-Water-Supply/tyen-gy62.

5 James Madison, *Federalist Papers #51* (1788), http://files.libertyfund.org/files/788/0084_LFeBk.pdf, p. 269.

6 "The Trump Administration Is Reversing Nearly 100 Environmental Rules," *New York Times*, Oct. 15, 2020, https://www.nytimes.com/interactive/2020/climate/trump-environment-rollbacks-list.html.

7 Boyce, *The Case for Carbon* Dividends, op. cit., p. 5.

8 The Politics of Universal Property

1 Nathan J. Russell, "An Introduction to the Overton Window of Political Possibilities" (2006), Mackinac Center for Public Policy, Midland MI, https://www.mackinac.org/7504.

2 John Locke, *Second Treatise of Government*, Ch. 5, Sec. 26.

3 Rupert Jones, "£9bn Bonanza Begins as Child Trust Funds Come of Age," *Guardian*, August 22, 2020, https://www.theguardian.com/money/2020/aug/22/9bn-bonanza-begins-as-child-trust-funds-come-of-age.

4 Citizens Basic Income Trust, https://citizensincome.org/; Royal Society for the Arts, https://www.thersa.org/projects/basic-income.

British books on basic income published within the last five years include Stewart Lansley, *A Sharing Economy* (2016), Policy Press, Bristol; Guy Standing, *Basic Income: And How We Can Make It Happen* (2017), Pelican Books, London; Malcolm Torry, *Why We Need a Citizen's Income* (2018), Policy Press, Bristol; and Louise Haagh, *The Case for Universal Basic Income* (2019), Polity, Cambridge.

5 On the impact of Meade's ideas see Stuart White, "Citizen Ownership: the Lost Radicalism of the Centre?," *Open*

Democracy, November 8, 2013, https://www. opendemocracy. net/en/opendemocracyuk/citizen-ownership-lost-radicalism -of-centre/.

6 https://positivemoney.org/.

7 Mankiw panacea quote, https://www.youtube.com/watch?v= emQRarafu_ s&feature=emb_title.

8 https://www.economist.com/special-report/2019/09/26/the-best-way-to-eradicate-poverty-in-america-is-to-focus-on-chil dren.

9 Hillary Rodham Clinton, *What Happened* (2017), Simon and Schuster, New York, p. 238.

10 Nathaniel Herz, "Undiminished at 90 Years Old, Clem Tillion Remains a Force in Juneau," *Anchorage Daily News,* January 27, 2016, https://www.adn.com/politics/article/90-years-old-undiminished-tillion-remains-force-juneau/2016/01/27/.

11 Bear in mind that Norway's assets are entirely financial and tradable, while the social wealth fund envisioned here would include non-tradable property rights (e.g. ecosystem conservation easements) with the capacity to generate income.

9 The Adjacent Possible

1 Niles Eldredge and Stephen Jay Gould, "Punctuated Equilibria: An Alternative to Phyletic Gradualism," in T. J. M. Schopf, ed., *Models in Paleobiology* (1972), Freeman Cooper, San Francisco, pp. 82–115, http://www.blackwellpublishing.com/ridley/clas sictexts/eldredge.pdf.

2 Stuart Kauffman, *Investigations* (2000), Oxford University Press, Oxford, p. 142 ff.

3 *With Liberty and Dividends for All* (2014), p. 94, in which I estimate potential revenue from various co-inherited assets. Also see the Appendix, p. 139 ff. I've since come to believe that these estimates were too low for the amount of Fed money that could safely be issued.

4 Milton Friedman, *Capitalism and Freedom* (1962), University of Chicago Press, Chicago, p. xiv, 2002 paperback edition.

5 Trevor Griffiths, *These Are the Times: A Life of Thomas Paine* (2004), Spokesman, Nottingham.

Select Bibliography

Many books address *pieces* of my argument; only a few address them all. In this selective bibliography, I've listed the full-spectrum books first, followed by a few classics and then books related to specific topics covered in this book. Within each category I've listed the books chronologically. Additional papers and articles can be found in the end notes.

Full spectrum

E. F. Schumacher, *Small is Beautiful: Economics as if People Mattered* (1973), Harper & Row, New York

Geoff Davies, *Economia* (2001), ABC Books, Sydney

Kate Haworth, *Doughnut Economics* (2017), Chelsea Green Publishing, White River Junction VT

Fraser Murison Smith, *A Planetary Economy* (2020), Palgrave Macmillan, London

Classics

Adam Smith, *An Inquiry into the Nature and Causes of the Wealth of Nations* (1776)

Thomas Paine, *Agrarian Justice* (1796)

Henry George, *Progress and Poverty* (1880)

Select Bibliography

Arthur C. Pigou, *The Economics of Welfare* (1920), Macmillan, London

John Maynard Keynes, *The General Theory of Employment, Interest and Money* (1936), Macmillan, London

Property rights

Daniel W. Bromley, *Environment and Economy: Property Rights and Public Policy* (1991), Blackwell, Oxford

Charles Geisler and Gail Daneker (eds.), *Property and Values: Alternative to Public and Private Ownership* (2000), Island Press, Washington DC

Sally Fairfax, and Jon Souder, *Conservation Trusts* (2001), University of Kansas Press, Lawrence KS

Guy Shrubsole, *Who Owns England?* (2019), William Collins, London

Common wealth

Elinor Ostom, *Governing the Commons* (1990), Cambridge University Press, New York

Peter Brown, *The Commonwealth of Life: A Treatise on Stewardship Economics* (2001), Black Rose Books, Montreal

David Bollier, *Silent Theft: The Private Plunder of our Common Wealth* (2002), Routledge, New York

Peter Barnes, *Capitalism 3.0: A Guide to Reclaiming the Commons* (2006), Berrett-Koehler, San Francisco

Jonathan Rowe, *Our Common Wealth: The Hidden Economy That Makes Everything Else Work* (2013), Berrett-Koehler, San Francisco

Dag Detter and Stefan Fölster, *The Public Wealth of Nations* (2015), Palgrave Macmillan, London

Select Bibliography

Guy Standing, *Plunder of the Commons: A Manifesto for Sharing Public Wealth* (2019), Pelican, London

Inequality

Richard Wilkinson and Kate Pickett, *The Spirit Level: Why Greater Equality Makes Societies Stronger* (2009), Penguin, London

Joseph E. Stiglitz, *The Price of Inequality: How Today's Divided Society Endangers Our Future* (2013), Norton, New York

Thomas Piketty, *Capital in the Twenty-first Century* (2014), Harvard University Press, Cambridge MA

Money, debt, and finance

Michael Rowbotham, *The Grip of Death: A Study of Modern Money, Debt Slavery and Destructive Economics* (1998), Jon Carpenter Publishing, Charlbury (UK)

Rana Foroohar, *Makers and Takers: How Wall Street Destroyed Main Street* (2016), Crown Business, New York

Randall Wray, *Why Minsky Matters* (2016), Princeton University Press, Princeton

Adair Turner, *Between Debt and the Devil: Money, Credit, and Fixing Global Finance* (2016), Princeton University Press, Princeton

Frances Coppola, *The Case For People's Quantitative Easing* (2019), Polity, Cambridge UK

Stephanie Kelton, *The Deficit Myth: Modern Monetary Theory and the Birth of the People's Economy* (2020), PublicAffairs, New York

Robert Hockett and Aaron James, *Money From Nothing* (2020), Melville House, Brooklyn

Select Bibliography

Markets and nature

John Dales, *Pollution, Property and Prices* (1968), University of Toronto Press, Toronto

James Lovelock, *Gaia: A New Look At Life on Earth* (1979), Oxford University Press, Oxford

James Lovelock, *Gaia: The Practical Science of Planetary Medicine* (1991), Gaia Books Limited, London

Herman Daly, *Beyond Growth: The Economics of Sustainable Development* (1996), Beacon Press, Boston

Geoffrey Heal, *Nature and the Marketplace: Capturing the Value of Ecosystem Services* (2000), Island Press, Washington

Paul Collier, *The Plundered Planet* (2010), Oxford University Press, Oxford

Basic income, social wealth funds, and inheritances

James Meade, *Efficiency, Equality and the Ownership of Property* (1964), Allen & Unwin, London

Robert Theobold (ed.), *The Guaranteed Income: Next Step in Socioeconomic Evolution?* (1966), Doubleday, New York

Bruce Ackerman and Anne Alstott, *The Stakeholder Society* (1999), Yale University Press, New Haven CT

Bill Gates Sr. and Chuck Collins, *Wealth and Our Commonwealth: Why America Should Tax Accumulated Fortunes* (2003), Beacon Press, Boston

Stuart White (ed.), *The Citizen's Stake: Exploring the Future of Universal Asset Policies* (2006), Policy Press, Bristol

Dwight Murphey, *A Shared Market Economy: A Classical Liberal Rethinks the Market System* (2009), Kindle

Select Bibliography

Peter Barnes, *With Liberty and Dividends for All* (2014), Berrett-Koehler, San Francisco

Stewart Lansley, *A Sharing Economy* (2016), Policy Press, Bristol

Philippe van Parijs and Yannick Vanderborght, *Basic Income: A Radical Proposal for a Free Society and a Sane Economy* (2017), Harvard University Press, Cambridge MA

Marcellus Andrews, *The Vision of a Real Free Market Society* (2017), Routledge, New York

Guy Standing, *Basic Income: And How We Can Make It Happen* (2017), Pelican Books, London

Malcolm Torry, *Why We Need a Citizen's Income* (2018), Policy Press, Bristol

Andrew Yang, *The War on Normal People: The Truth About America's Disappearing Jobs and Why Universal Basic Income Is Our Future* (2018), Hachette Books, New York

Louise Haagh, *The Case for Universal Basic Income* (2019), Polity, Cambridge UK

The economy as a complex system

Philip Ball, *Critical Mass: How One Thing Leads to Another* (2004), Arrow, London

Eric D. Beinhocker, *The Origin of Wealth* (2006), Harvard Business School Press, Boston

David Collander, *Complexity and the History of Economic Thought* (2008), Middlebury College, Middlebury VT

Index

Page numbers in *italics* refer to figures.

Index

Index

Index

Index